THE NIGHT-SIDE

THE NIGHT-SIDE

Chronic Fatigue Syndrome
and the Illness Experience

Floyd Skloot

Story Line Press
1996

Story Line Press; Three Oaks Farm; Brownsville, OR 97327
Printed in Canada

This publication was made possible thanks in part to the generous support of the Nicholas Roerich Museum, the Andrew W. Mellon
Foundation, the National Endowment for the Arts, and our individual
contributors.

Book design by Chiquita Babb

Library of Congress Cataloging-in-Publication Data
Skloot, Floyd.
    The night-side : chronic fatigue syndrome and the illness
experience / Floyd Skloot.
        p. cm.
    ISBN 1-885266-31-6
        1. Skloot, Floyd—Health.   2. Chronic fatigue syndrome—
Patients—United States—Biography. I. Title.
    RB150.F37S58 1996
    362.1'96047—dc20
    [B]   96-8218
                                                                      CIP

"Illness is the night-side of life, a more onerous citizenship. Everyone who is born holds dual citizenship, in the kingdom of the well and in the kingdom of the sick."

—Susan Sontag, from *Illness as Metaphor*

For Beverly

Acknowledgments

Grateful acknowledgment is made to the editors of the following magazines, where parts of this book first appeared: *The American Scholar, The Antioch Review, Boulevard, Changing Men, Common Journeys, Commonweal, Crazyhorse, The Gettysburg Review, The Iowa Review, JAMA: The Journal of the American Medical Association, Northeast Corridor, Poetry Northwest, The Portland Oregonian, Prairie Schooner, Runner's World, South Dakota Review, St. Petersburg Times, The Sun, Threepenny Review, Tracks (Ireland), The Virginia Quarterly Review, Voices, and Willamette Week.*

"Trivia Tea: Baseball as Balm" was reprinted in *The Best American Essays of 1993*, edited by Joseph Epstein, (NY: Ticknor & Fields). "Home Remedies" is reprinted from *The American Scholar*, Vol.64, No. 1, (Winter 1995), by permission of the publishers. "Honeymooning with the Feminine Divine" is reprinted by permission from *The Antioch Review*, Vol. 53, No. 2 (Spring 1995). "Trivia Tea: Baseball as Balm" originally appeared in *The Gettysburg Review*, Vol. 5, No. 3 (Summer 1992), and is reprinted here by permission of the editors.

I want to thank the Oregon Arts Commission and Oregon Literary Arts, Inc., for fellowships, and Centrum and the Villa Montalvo for residencies during the time this book was written. I also want to thank my family and friends for their loyal support.

Contents

Preface

I know it was nothing personal. I know I was simply a host the virus used to do the only thing it knew how to do, enact its sole pattern of growth. I was like a windowpane latticed with crystals of snow, simply present at the critical moment when the storm came along. From the virus's point of view, I could have been a stone, or a broth of monkey kidneys and Medium 199 as in the most sophisticated laboratory, a block of moss. Or I could have been you.

It was a matter of being as good as the next available body. Perhaps I was worn down at the wrong moment, perhaps I was missing the proper envelope of protein, but it was nothing more essential about the self than that. Tired of my busy life, a war zone of forces besieging the fortress of who I am? Spare me metaphor. As Susan Sontag says on the first page of her book *Illness as Metaphor*, "My point is that illness is *not* a metaphor, and the most truthful way of regarding illness—and the healthi-est way of being ill—is one most purified of, most resistant to, metaphoric thinking." I buy that, and the book you are about to read starts from the assumption that illness must be looked at straight-on, in all its implications. It also explores that wild co-nundrum of Sontag's about the healthiest way of being ill.

Reality, illness teaches you, is filled with such contradictions. It may seem surprising, even threatening, that when I got sick I was in the best physical shape of my life, a prize-winning long distance racer avid about diet and weight. This glowing state of health did nothing to protect me after all. The virus didn't care. It didn't even need me to live because without me it would still be there, the way viruses are, in their land of limbo, never quite dead enough to forget, never quite alive enough to kill.

So it wasn't personal, yet I had no choice but to take it personally. I did not misbehave, did not court disaster. Nevertheless, I have lived seven years in a protracted cold war (all right, an occasional metaphor, but about how illness feels, not about what it means). I have been occupied by an unseen enemy—the virus — who is a master saboteur, and my secret codes have been broken. Little works the way it was programmed to work. I have lost control over my body, its order has been shattered and pockets of resistance crushed one by one. From time to time, all-out war threatens; I feel as though I'm being torn apart like an atom bombarded. That's the way these invaders work in the body, no lie.

Personally, then, I have become other, different from what I was, though it was never personal. I have seen my body become a factory of disease in this occupied country, spewing internal acid rain and polluting the very lifestream that coursed its way through me. Slowly the banks of my old self eroded, each lush growth that fed there turning sere.

I began writing this book in late 1989, almost a year after getting sick, and finished it in the middle of 1995. But *The Night-Side* is not the chronological story of my ongoing experience with illness. Nor is it a book about my specific illness. What happened to me is not terribly different from what happens to people who contract lupus, multiple sclerosis, cardiovascular disease, arthritis, emphysema, scleroderma or any other chronic illness. Instead, this book is a meditation forwards and backwards over the losses and gains that accompany long-term illness. Some of its pieces follow one another like chapters in a novel, others connect more associatively, like poems in a collection. It is finally an account of change and, I think, growth.

PART ONE

Into Darkness

"Not every man knows what is waiting for him, or what
  he shall sing
When the ship he is on slips into darkness"

—Mark Strand, from "The End"

1

An Unbelievable Illness

THERE'S A LOT wrong with me. My spinal fluid contains twice as much protein as it should. My brain is swollen and scarred, my IQ deteriorating, my visual memory in shambles. If I see you scratch your head while I'm talking to you, chances are I'll forget what I'm trying to say. Even if I remember, it probably won't come out the way I planned. Often I can't find the words that I need, or I use words bizarrely: in complaining that my hair has been thinning, I say that my hair was leaking. I walk along the garlic driveway instead of the gravel driveway. My sunglasses are storm catchers.

I begin to write not knowing if I'm going to be able to do this at all. Since my thought processes are so weirdly disrupted, since I can't concentrate well or for long and memory is highly variable, I rely on scattered notes. But I can't spell anymore (words come out all twisted up: *crhnoic* instead of *chronic*, *does* instead of *dose*), so reading those notes is often difficult and distressing. My ability to think abstractly is compromised, so I work from very specific points and hope to see later on how they link together. What my neuropsychologist has called "difficulty in keeping track of ongoing mental activity," I experience as being estranged from my normally reliable mind. Cut off against my will, as though it had walked out on me and left no forwarding address.

Researchers at their lab benches in Maryland can cultivate several different viruses from my blood and spinal fluid, demonstrating that those viruses are rampant in my body. I have test results that indicate my body's defense mechanism, the immune system, has no response to common viral material introduced in a skin test—antigens for mumps, tetanus, candida—that ought to drive it berserk. At the same time, other tests reveal that components of my immune system's antiviral pathways measure abnormally high and most of the system is hyperactive. So for years I've continually had all the intense flu-like symptoms of a body waging a futile war with foreign invaders. The tests taken together show that my immune system is both energized and sluggish, parts of it working overtime and other parts on strike.

My central nervous system is where the worst results of this interior toxic spill show themselves. Trying to wash a soup pot in the kitchen sink, I've extended the rinsing hose and pointed its nozzle down the neck of my shirt instead of into the pot, drenching and astonishing myself in an instant. I've put talcum powder instead of Crest on my toothbrush, banana peels in the freezer for composting, ice cubes in the cupboard, and a salad in the oven to cool. I get lost walking streets I've walked for years and have become the world's most unreliable map reader. When I accompany my wife to the grocery store, there's a significant question about whether I'll actually pick out what I'm looking for. A stock clerk chatted with me while I was selecting Santa Rosas and I put my bag of plums into the recycling bin instead of our cart—an interesting variation on my usual theme of depositing the goods I select into other shoppers' carts. Although I was a collegiate baseball player and a lifelong jock, my balance is unpredictable now, as is my coordination. I break mugs, plates and glass cookware so often that I no longer risk clean-up duty. I see obstacles in my path and walk into them anyway. For nearly a decade, I had been a daily runner, putting in more than 2,000 miles a year along densely wooded trails. Now, instead of alternating Nike and Saucony running shoes every day, I alternate hand-carved canes and replace their black rubber tips every six months.

All of which says little about how I feel. Most often, I feel unplugged, as though the cables to my fuel sources have been shredded. At times I feel unmoored, the vessel of my self having slipped from its anchorage to my body. And although I resist it, sometimes I simply feel unhealthy, like a polluted stream. The glands in my neck have been tender to the touch since 1988, my eyelids and upper lip often flutter, my eyes and mouth are so dry they tend to stick shut. When my joints and muscles merely ache as though I've just run a dozen hilly miles, they're feeling better than usual. I can no longer reach to scratch my back. I have dreams in which a giant stalk of rotten celery is growing out of my mouth. When I try to pull it free, the thing is rooted so deeply in my belly that it feels as though I am uprooting my soul.

But I look all right, even if my tightly curled ethnic hair has straightened and my muscles, built up by years of hard training, have lost all tone. Not far removed from running a handful of back-to-back five and a half minute miles, I now buckle after seven minutes of easy walking during an exercise treadmill test, breathless and fatigued. Sitting in a chair afterward to recover from the exertion, ten electrodes still stuck to my shaven torso, I can only stare at the floor and wonder about the body's essential delicacy—I, who always thought of my body as sturdy, almost indomitable.

And the things I say! I ask a friend for a stick of decaffeinated gum, ask my doctor whether the blood tests show amnesia instead of anemia, call the car's antenna an umbrella, and my Greek captain's hat a shiptain's hat. I say that film needs to be validated instead of developed. The Xerox machine apparently stands for all machines in my rearranged brain: I ask my wife to reheat my coffee in the Xerox, ask my son to Xerox the lawn, explain to my daughter that the doctor will Xerox her injured arm. My math has become utterly original, which makes for some interesting challenges with the check book and the IRS returns. It's as though my brain has been rewired by Gracie Allen.

This is not the way I was before.

I have Chronic Fatigue Syndrome (CFS). Also known as Chronic Fatigue and Immune Dysfunction Syndrome (CFIDS) or Chronic Epstein-Barr Virus (CEBV) and perhaps soon to be known as Chronic Immune Activation Syndrome (CIAS), Acquired Immuno-neurological Syndrome (AINS) or Florence Nightingale's Disease. If I hear you call it the Yuppie Flu, I'll hit you with a Xerox machine.

According to one prominent physician familiar with the disease, Dr. Jay Levy of San Francisco, CFS is "the disease of the '90s." It is, Levy means, the disease of the '90s as AIDS was the disease of the '80s. In part, this is because of the sheer numbers involved: two to five million Americans afflicted; the Centers for Disease Control in Atlanta getting 1,000 to 2,000 phone inquiries about the disease each month; hundreds of thousands of the more severely ill people being forced to leave their jobs because of its symptoms. But CFS is also the disease of the '90s in the same way that, perhaps, nuclear waste disposal is the environmental issue of the '90s or taxation is the political issue of the '90s: because of the magnitude of costs involved in addressing them, because of how long and willfully they have been ignored as problems, because of the implications of not solving them.

◆

I GOT SICK on December 7, 1988, my personal "Day of Infamy." As Thanksgiving approached, I was 41 and fitter than ever, running seven or eight miles a day at 5:30 A.M. A serious competitive racer, I was winning ribbons in my age group nearly every weekend in 5Ks, 8Ks and 10Ks. Throughout summer and early fall, I'd trained intensively and broken personal records at every distance from one mile to the marathon.

I'd just completed a second novel and third chapbook of poems. My new writing was appearing in magazines like *Harper's*, the *New Criterion, Shenandoah,* and *Prairie Schooner.* I was awarded a poetry fellowship by the Oregon Institute of Literary Arts and received a prize for my fiction from the Kansas Arts Commission/Kansas Quarterly, was giving readings every few months and began teaching a poetry writing class in my home one evening a week.

At work, where I was Senior Public Policy Analyst for a diversified energy corporation, I'd gotten a bonus and raise for my performance during the last legislative session and had been given new responsibilities. It was common for me to be on the phone dealing simultaneously with questions on proposed legislation in Oregon, Washington, California, Montana, Idaho and Wyoming; people were waiting for my advice before acting.

On December 7, I was in Washington D.C. at an energy policy seminar. I woke to run at 6:00 A.M. (3:00 A.M. body time, since I live in Oregon), but something was wrong. The room reeked, as though I could smell the odors of everyone who'd ever stayed there, and I was too exhausted to fold back the sheets. I felt dizzy and disoriented, walking into walls, trying to enter the elevator before the doors opened. Jet lag, I thought; this can't stop me. So I forced myself out of bed, had to concentrate in order to tie my shoes, and went out to run two laps around the Mall. After all, I had a race back home Sunday morning and needed the workout.

I couldn't stay awake during the seminar. I had no desire for dinner, though I'd looked forward to eating at an Indian restaurant that a friend recommended. I took a cab to a nearby bookstore instead of walking there. Back at the hotel, though deeply tired, I couldn't sleep and went down to the bar for a ten dollar snifter of cognac. I couldn't take one sip—alcohol suddenly seemed disgusting.

Sudden onset, consistent with viral infection, is a classic symptom of CFS. The baffling speed with which my power was stripped —and never returned—remains shocking more than seven years later. As Dr. Oliver Sacks says in his book *A Leg To Stand On,* "To be full of strength and vigor one moment and virtually helpless the next, in the pink and pride of health one moment and a cripple the next, with all one's powers and faculties one moment and without them the next—such a change, such suddenness, is difficult to comprehend, and the mind casts about for explanations."

But not right away, because I was too severely affected even to realize how sick I was. By Christmas, I couldn't concentrate at work, was having trouble reading, had run out of ideas. I got lost trying to find my way back from the coffee shop I'd gone to every day for two years. I could no longer remember people's names, explain how a hydroelectric dam works, articulate why the proposed merger with Utah Power would benefit our ratepayers. I kept reversing numbers when I did math and letters when I wrote, so that my memos and cost projections were consistently incorrect. I couldn't spell. Although I didn't feel feverish, I decided to take my temperature one day. It was 96.2 and remained below 97 for the next seven years. I was sleeping no more than two consecutive hours. I had agonizing headaches; they were pinpointed between my eyes and would last for five days, untouchable by any analgesic. My leg muscles and joints always hurt, as though I'd just run a marathon. This was confusing because I could barely run a mile anymore.

Listen to your body, my running friends always said. Listen to your body, I told friends who were hurt. I listened, heard my body saying it was fatigued, and decided to push harder in order to break through. Running was synonymous with health; so if I forced myself to keep running, I would get stronger and beat this thing, which seemed like the most tenacious flu I'd ever had. When I went to the bathroom, I wasn't sure I'd be able to make it back to the bedroom without stopping for a rest.

It took till January 20 before I finally could not get out of bed at all. My body was shot, my mind was shot, and my head was so disconnected from my body that I still thought a couple of nights' sleep would do it. My family convinced me that this was more than flu to the fifth power.

✦

IT TOOK five months to get diagnosed with CFS. From January through May 1989, my former wife and I went to a half dozen doctors in search of an explanation for my deteriorating health. She would take me to appointments for tests or consultations, would pick up x-rays and films of brain scans so they would appear at the right doctor's office at the right time. I could not have done it without her help, in part because I was no longer able to drive and in part because I was unable to explain my symptoms or history coherently. She helped convey my situation to skeptical doctors as well as taking notes so that we could make sense of what they were saying. She dealt with insurance carriers and the personnel office of my employer. Most important, she believed in me.

I heard a scaresome medley of preliminary diagnoses: it might be hepatitis, Lyme's disease brought on by a tick bite in the woods where I ran, multiple and amyotrophic lateral sclerosis, somatization disorder (it was all in my head). I was tested for AIDS, syphilis, leukemia, and cancer. I heard a new language, in which doctors spoke of unremarkable tests, though some were pretty remarkable to me, of insidious onset, morbidity and elevated titers. I encountered indifferent machines and technicians, swallowed awful potions and was injected with fluids that felt both hot and cold at the same time. I was probed, biopsied and drained. I went through tests that could only have been designed by someone much sicker than I was. About the only thing the medical practitioners seemed not to be doing was listening to me.

In his book *Newton's Madness: Further Tales of Clinical Neurology*, Dr. Harold L. Klawans says, "It is fear that leads physicians to rely more on scientific data than on their patients. Laboratory results, not history. X rays, not the physical examination. Logic, not insight. And never intuition. And along the way, understanding and caring have gotten lost." Norman Cousins extends this point in *Anatomy of an Illness*, when he says "some doctors tend to favor the new technology precisely because they don't have time enough to allow the diagnosis to emerge from a comprehensive direct personal examination, and from extended give-and-take with the patient." Cousins also talks about the laying on of hands having been replaced by the laying on of tools. Dr. Oliver Sacks in *Awakenings* talks about the difficulty "created by physicians themselves who, in effect, decline to listen to their patients, to treat them as equals, and who are prone to adopt—from force of habit, or from a less excusable sense of professional apartness and superiority—an approach and language which effectively prevent any real communication between themselves and their patients." That's certainly the way it was for me as I witnessed the art of healing disappearing within the science of diagnosis.

I endured a battery of the most sophisticated and expensive procedures, including brain and liver scans, magnetic resonance imaging, a lumbar puncture, electroencephalography and electromyography. This last procedure, where the doctor jabs huge needles into your muscles to measure their ability to conduct electrical impulses, all the while murmuring "most patients tell me this doesn't hurt," is given +++ out of a possible ++++ on the pain intensity scale by the book *Medical Tests and Diagnostic Procedures* and is dourly deemed "an experience that is totally aversive."

I failed to put together simple jigsaw puzzles or count backwards from a hundred by sevens and could not stand erect with my feet together and eyes closed. I had to work very hard to get my index finger to touch my nose.

Even with my memory in tatters, it will be hard to forget the first physician I went to, Dr. Felix. He stood at the foot of the examination table, mumbling to himself as he read instructions for a Thyroid Releasing Hormone Test, which he said he had never performed before. His wife, who was also the nurse, attempted to distract me by asking about my family, but I was transfixed by the sight of this man trying to figure out how to conduct a test he said would cause my blood pressure to fluctuate wildly, make me flash hot, and cause me to feel an intense need to urinate for its entire thirty-minute duration. His demeanor, especially when he crumpled up the page in frustration, suggested nothing so much as my son when he was a boy, hating to read instructions and preferring to "figure it out by doing it." I'd already upset him by falling asleep on his examining table while waiting for him and, when I jerked awake, knocking to the floor and cracking a plastic valve on the blood pressure gauge he had left beside me. His wife ushered Dr. Felix out of the room after that happened so he could calm down before returning to undertake the test.

Or Dr. Mudgett, bearded and a former athlete who looked enough like me to be a brother. First he refused to meet my eyes as he told me he was convinced I was not depressed and not presenting myself as ill in order to gain sympathy, time off from work, or inappropriate access to disability funds. Next he told me I might be suffering from a post-viral fatigue of unknown origin and—if I was—that there was nothing he could offer me to manage it. Then he told me I should see someone more qualified to interpret a potential psychological overlay to my complaints and left the room before I could challenge him to explain how—if all he'd said about me were true—my illness could have a psychological overlay other than what these doctors were causing.

Eventually, I was lucky. First I found a doctor who said, essentially, "all the things that are wrong with you aren't the thing that's wrong with you, they're caused by the thing that's wrong with you.". Then he sent me to Dr. Mark Loveless in May of 1989. Loveless, whose surname sounds like a Victorian novelist's moniker for the Physician from Hell, knew exactly what was wrong with me. Bad as the diagnosis was—a disease that could neither be treated nor cured—I wept with relief at having a name for it.

✦

IN PART, the diagnosis was so hard to come by because I got sick a few years too early. Now, in 1995, far more is known about CFS and it is being taken more seriously by the medical community. At a press conference in the fall of 1990, when the discovery of a leukemia-like retrovirus was announced as being potentially associated with CFS, Dr. Paul Cheney had this to say about patients with the disease: "you see their entire social structure, work interactions and family units come crashing down over the several years that can typically affect these patients before they begin to recover somewhat." With grand and, I believe unconscious ambiguity, he added: "*It is an unbelievable illness.*"

Maybe part of the problem is the name. Calling this Chronic Fatigue Syndrome is as inadequate as calling emphysema Chronic Coughing Syndrome—it highlights one symptom and doesn't touch the reality of the disease. And labeling it the Yuppie Flu is as misleading and demeaning as labeling Parkinson's Disease the Geriatric Shakes. In Great Britain, CFS is known as Myalgic Encephalomyelitis, a name with heft, the kind that might earn the disease greater respect in America. But until the gravity of the disease is fully accepted, the media would most likely seize on its acronym (the ME Disease?) to create as unflattering an image as it has with the Yuppie Flu.

One reason medical research can't settle on a name is that it hasn't identified a specific cause or pathology (for example, the way *poliomyelitis* means gray marrow). Another part of the reason is that the symptoms are so diverse and disparate it's hard to find a label stretching wide enough to fit (in the way that *arthritis* means joint inflammation). But the primary reason its name remains at issue is that the act of naming is an act of recognition. It really isn't surprising that this disease has had a hard time in America. As of now, it cannot be definitively diagnosed through technological means—using blood and other laboratory tests, x-rays, brain scans, MRIs—and these are the means to which our medical practitioners typically adhere. If they can't find it with machines, it doesn't exist. Further, recognizing this disease as legitimate has serious political and economic implications. Research would have to be funded adequately. Government agencies and private insurance carriers would have to acknowledge it, would have to respond appropriately to it and support its victims. As with AIDS, which was originally spoken of as the gay cancer if it was spoken of at all, CFS can be denied by assigning it pejorative labels or names that diminish its seriousness, implying that its victims somehow are getting what their lifestyle warrants.

✦

IT IS A stroke of good fortune that I had the support and trust of my family, many friends, and colleagues from work. After I got sick, a friend I used to run and race with visited me at least twice a week. Eric used my home as his health club, changing for runs along the same wooded trails we once ran together, cooling down in my living room while we talked. It was wonderful, as though my illness had changed nothing between us except my ability to be beside him on the trails.

A few people I used to work with, colleagues from the public policy group that the rest of the utility company referred to as Arts & Crafts, would call at least three times a week. They sometimes brought lunch to me and spent their hour at the round oak table in my dining room. They stopped asking under what names I stored various memos on my word processor at the office because I couldn't remember, but they continued to make me feel present and important in their lives.

My two children, although grown and living outside the home, busy in their new adult lives, kept in touch almost daily. They progressed with me through the typical stages of denial, fear, anger, acceptance; they are simply there for me. It is a source of joy to draw from. My former wife remained committed to my support during the last four years of our marriage, which ended in divorce in 1992. CFS forced us to redefine completely the familiar division of responsibilities that governed the first two decades of our life together. I could no longer do what I did, the family's cooking and laundry, the petty errands, the driving, the tax returns. We had to sell our home—because I had trouble climbing the stairs to go to the bathroom, because my income was radically reduced, because her new job involved a hundred-mile daily commute—and I couldn't carry my customary load in all that a relocation entailed. Probably more than all the newly assumed duties and shlepping, what meant the most was that she didn't make me feel like a burden to her. I wonder sometimes if I'd have had the moxie to do as well if the situation were reversed.

✦

I TRIED EVERYTHING there was to try. If it had been written about in *The CFIDS Chronicle*, an invaluable journal published by the Chronic Fatigue and Immune Dysfunction Syndrome Association in Charlotte, NC, I tried it. If it had been talked about in my support groups or over my informal national phone network, and didn't involve voodoo, I considered it.

I learned that with a disease for which there's no known treatment or cure, you'll try almost anything. The hardest thing is to do nothing, to go home and rest, which is what most of the doctors I saw suggested. My doctor, fortunately, was among the few nationwide who had worked with CFS and kept up with current research.

Because my immunoglobulin titers were low, and because it had been anecdotally reported to help, we tried intramuscular shots of immunoglobulin. Every two weeks for four months during the late spring and early summer, I came up to the clinic to see his nurse, who was a dead ringer for the actress Teri Garr. Seven months pregnant and gleaming with good humor, she rubbed the syringe between her hands. Immunoglobulin is thick as toothpaste; she was warming it for me, softening it. This was the stuff they used in the fifties to try and ward off polio attacks if people had been exposed to the virus. It was a notoriously painful injection and she was doing all she could to ease that pain.

The shots didn't help. We tried small doses of Naltrexone, a drug that's often used to help addicts going through detox because it blocks the effects of such drugs as opium and morphine. The theory behind its use on me was that it also stimulates the endorphin receptors and has a positive effect on immune cells. It was a sweet red liquid I kept beside the tabasco sauce in our refrigerator. It didn't help either.

We tried the standard CFS therapy, a wide array of antidepressants taken in lower than normal doses, which didn't improve my condition but seemed to bring all my bodily functions to a halt. I could sleep through the night when I was taking them, but I could barely wake up all day. We abandoned the antidepressants and tried such sleeping aids as chloral hydrate because, despite my exhaustion, I was unable to sleep for more than two hours at a time. We tried antibiotics. My doctor explained the concept of "aggressive rest" to me, screwing my mind around to where I could view bed rest as an active form of therapy rather than as doing nothing. Some of the literature appearing in regard to CFS talked about the clear link between this disease and the development of certain cancers, particularly lymphomas (a recent book entitled *What Really Killed Gildna Radner* uses this issue to intensify its claim that CFS is a potentially fatal disease). So doing nothing was a terrifying thought. I considered massive doses of magnesium and vitamin C. I agreed to participate in a two-month experiment using intravenous and oral doses of DMSO, a controversial therapy that is perhaps most famous for its positive results with pain in horses.

I tried acupuncture for several months, lying there with needles stuck in my face and neck, my chest, my toes. It seemed to make me more exhausted, though it did relieve my headache if I had one on the day of treatment and being in the presence of the practitioner was soothing.

I participated in an experimental fourteen-week program assembled by Oregon Health Sciences University for a half dozen of us. It combined occupational therapy, nutritional and psychological counseling, relaxation techniques, and group interaction in an attempt to teach us to live more effectively with our illness. We were tested at the beginning and end of the program to determine whether we'd benefitted from participating. After fourteen weeks, I still couldn't march up and down the stairs at the acceptable pace or perform the memory exercises properly or sleep for more than two hours at a time.

By the end of fifteen months, I had exhausted the options.

I never imagined that I'd be a medical research subject. Let doctors conduct experiments on my body? Well, maybe to find out why my performances as a runner kept getting better once I passed forty. Floyd the Medical Marvel, I would graciously let them study that. Put me on a treadmill and watch me run for hours. But certainly not to find out whether some new, synthetic chemical was safe and effective in treating a dysfunctional immune system. That was for other people. It's astonishing how quickly serious illness can rearrange your imagination. It's astonishing to what lengths you will go in an effort to find a cure for an incurable disease.

2

Double Blind

"Concern for the interests of the subject must always prevail over the interests of science and society."
— The Physician's Oath of the World Medical Association

WELCOME TO THE Solarium. It's always this warm in here, even with the blinds drawn, even with all the Oregon rain.

That machine in the corner is hooked up to a blind man snoozing in the next room. It knows when he enters deep sleep and warns the nurse to jolt him awake. Every hour or so, I see him walk down the hallway, hand against the tile wall, and turn back when he reaches those swinging double doors that separate the rest of University Hospital from our Clinical Research Center.

The elderly man to my right wearing a leather snap-brim cap is sitting on his hand because he's trying to hide Parkinsonian tremors. He listens distractedly to the young woman asking questions.

"Do your symptoms make you irritable?"

"No, Goddamnit!"

The man in overalls and slippers who cannot hear is watching "The Price Is Right" while he waits for his morning meal. An indwelling catheter is strapped to the crook of his elbow so his blood can be drawn as soon as he's finished eating. From time to time, you can see him look away from the television and stare at the catheter as though trying to measure which is worthier of attention.

I have come to hate "The Price Is Right," which I loved above all other game shows when I was ten. My mother used to watch it with me on Monday evenings, guessing the price of a new Amana range or baby Grand, a trip abroad. She had a cousin who was a buyer for the show, so she saw herself as virtually part of the cast. But now in the Solarium "The Price Is Right" drives me nuts. The beeper that signals an end to a segment is identical to the alarm sounded by my infusion pump whenever there's a blockage in the line. The alarm sounds often because these Volumetric Pumps are cheap; vacuums get created in the tubing, which causes the pumps to stop, the alarm to sound, and sometimes blood to be sucked out of my arm into the tubing. I get very uncomfortable when my blood turns the tubing pink and bubbly as Pepto-Bismol. So despite the beige recliner and the pillow cushioning my elbow, it's almost impossible to relax during "The Price Is Right" because I'm repeatedly convinced by the beeper that air bubbles are being infused into my veins. But we can't turn the show off; it's the favorite of that choleric patient with Parkinson's.

✦

I'VE BEEN a medical research subject for two years now. A human guinea pig.

This was not something I went into blindly. Human experimentation is an explosive topic, even when it's not being conducted on your own body. Nazis! Mad Scientists! Helpless patients injected with live cancer cells! I read about the development of the Nuremberg Code of medical practices, which established the principle of informed consent. I read about the 1964 Declaration of Helsinki, which established the basic principles that guide physicians in biomedical research on human subjects, and I studied the rules governing controlled clinical drug trials. I'd looked at reproductions of Rembrandt's gory 1632 painting, "The Anatomical Lesson," with the skin on the patient's left arm and hand peeled so that the researchers could see how stretching its tendons made the hand move. I also read the story of Alexis St. Martin, a teenaged French-Canadian fur trapper who was shot in the belly in 1822, and William Beaumont, the physician who saved him. Beaumont convinced his patient to permit the cleaned and dressed wound to remain open so that he could study the young man's digestive process, and entered into a contract binding St. Martin for one year in return for board, lodging and $150. Beaumont's experiments involved giving St. Martin food, watching the way his stomach reacted, and taking samples from the open wound. He wrote up his findings, published as "The Physiology of Digestion." Sensibly enough, St. Martin ran away as soon as he could. When he died, he was buried in secret by relatives who feared Beaumont would dig him up for further experimentation.

Did I want any part of this? Did I want to insist that my doctor, like the great researchers of the nineteenth century, try the drug out on himself first?

To me, there never really was a choice. Since I have an illness for which there is no cure or treatment, an illness so misunderstood that it had been virtually ignored by most medical practitioners and researchers, I was quite willing to offer myself for the study of an experimental drug as soon as I heard about it. Willing? I'd have done anything to get in.

✦

SINCE HIS FACE looks as though it would never need a shave, Dr. Mark Loveless's thick moustache seems like it must be glued on. In his white lab coat and stethoscope, he calls to mind a boy playing dress-up and, despite his clinical skepticism, appears cloaked in innocence.

I'm sure that's something he's had to deal with as long as he's been in practice. Loveless was virtually a real-life Doogie Howser. Since the sixth grade, when he catalogued all infectious diseases that had caused major outbreaks through history, he knew he wanted to be a doctor. In junior high, when I was riveted by the Hardy Boys, he was reading Berton Roueche's *Eleven Blue Men*, a book about epidemiologists.

Loveless is 41. But early enough in the day—before his office fills with the AIDS patients who comprise most of his Infectious Diseases practice—you'd guess he was half that. He's gentle, almost shy in the examining room, with a milky voice and sweet smile. But as lead guitarist for the rock group Windfall, he sings a fierce "Born to Be Wild" on the Bar Mitzvah and wedding circuit. He has an edge, thank heavens.

When I met him in May 1989, Loveless put me at ease. He was the first physician who'd done that in the five months it took to get my strange illness diagnosed. His uncle is the brother-in-law of a life-long friend of my ex-wife's father back in Illinois, though we didn't know that at the time. Hell, we were practically family. Standing close to me, looking in my eyes when he talked, he touched me on the arms and it felt neither forced nor generic. The man knew what was wrong with me and cared. I trusted him.

"We're gonna get you well," he said.

I believed him. I still do.

✦

MORE THAN a year later, in July 1990, Loveless stood before two dozen sick people in a room borrowed from Oregon Health

Sciences University's Pediatrics Department. Most of us sat slumped in our chairs or reclined on the floor. Next to Loveless on the desk, like a stack of test papers, were clean copies of forms —Patient Consent for Participation in Medical Research. We were evaluating whether to sign. I was glad he'd brought clean forms; I'd had to mark my copies up using four different colors of ink in a frantic effort to comprehend and retain what they said.

As of that summer day, Loveless was not exactly my doctor anymore and I was not his patient. He was a Researcher and I was his Subject. The distinction is acutely important. For a doctor, by oath the patient comes first. For a researcher, the product—a drug, a specimen, a protocol—comes first. I was being studied, not treated.

The room was so hidden among the labyrinthine corridors of the old hospital that most of us got lost trying to find our way there. Loveless was answering questions about the clinical field trial of a new drug that might treat our illness, a trial we had waited for months to begin. We'd have all remaining questions answered and doubts allayed.

"What happens at the end of the study?" he was asked. "Is the drug going to continue to be available?"

"Yeah. A second study is going to be backed up onto this one where everybody gets the drug."

"So it won't just stop?"

"No, that's unethical. We can't do that."

He was asked for further clarification. How long would we get the drug? Would it continue to be provided for free? He was growing impatient.

"Because it's unethical to stop an effective drug prior to marketing, the open label phases of these tests go until the drug is licensed. That has been the ethical thing to do. Now a few companies have decided not to do that. All I can tell you is that we're advocating as researchers that those people who are receiving benefit from this drug should be continued on and have it paid for by the company until it becomes licensed and available.

Since I'm not part of the company, I can't tell you that that's what's going to happen."

"I find that real risky," one of the patients said. "Say I get placebo for six months. But the study's real successful, and everybody gets the drug for another six months, and then the study's over . . ."

"No no no. That second study's open ended. There is no determined end point on that."

"So who determines when it ends?"

"It ends when the FDA approves the drug and it becomes licensed."

"And there won't be any charge during that time?"

"Right."

He looked at his watch. It wasn't difficult to read his mind. *How can it only be 12:30?*

The deal seemed straightforward and worth the risks. I'd let them experiment on my body with this new drug and if it worked, I would get the drug for free until it was approved for distribution. That's what the man said. Sign me up.

By signing the patient consent form, I entered into a contract. I understood that it would bind me to this clinical field trial for the duration, but felt the benefits were worth the risks.

✦

FIVE MONTHS prior to that meeting, having already been sick for more than a year, having tried everything available as treatment, I felt like a mountaineer lost in a storm. Every way I looked seemed the same as the way I'd been, and the footing was growing slick. Then there was sudden hope.

I was invited to participate in the randomized clinical field trial of a new drug that had treated seven of ten patients seriously ill with CFS in Nevada. Like a lot of other CFS patients, I'd been hearing rumors about this drug for months. There was something out there that made people better! Over a period from three to twelve months, these patients had shown improved performance on treadmill exercise testing and a reduction in symptoms of brain dysfunction on neurological testing. Preliminary results, but researchers and clinicians were encouraged. It was time to test whether the stuff really worked. Count me in.

The drug was called Ampligen, which sounded positively electric to me. It had been developed by a small company in Philadelphia, HEM Pharmaceuticals Corporation. The deal they were offering was simple to understand. If I were one of the 120 people accepted into the trial nationwide, I would be given either Ampligen or a placebo for six months. If the drug were proven to be effective in that time, I would be placed at once in a second phase of the study and given the drug until Ampligen was approved by the FDA for general distribution. It would be provided free of charge. This was important, because no insurance company would pay for the use of an experimental drug and its cost was estimated at up to $4,000 a month, which was certainly beyond the means of someone living—as the patients sick enough to qualify would have to be—on disability or welfare payments.

I had read that the director of the National Institute of Allergy and Infectious Diseases, Dr. Anthony Fauci, described the goal of a randomized clinical trial this way: "It's not to deliver therapy. It's to answer a scientific question so that the drug can be available for everybody once you've established safety and efficacy." Sure, guys, I get it. You're after knowledge, not curing Floyd Skloot. But the drug's mine after six months, right? Count me in.

I also heard that Ampligen was administered intravenously, like the solution I'd received upon collapsing after the Chicago Marathon in 1983. It was not something I could take as a pill or shot. I already knew I could deal with an I.V. There would be a huge commitment of my time and energy to receive the stuff twice a week, to go through rigorous testing procedures, to fill out paperwork. But my eyes were on the prize: get the drug, get better, get back my life. Count me in.

As soon as Loveless mentioned the Ampligen trial, I began

preparing myself to participate. He'd said I would not be allowed to use any other medications during the trial and suggested that I ought to begin living without them now, months before the screening and selection process began. That wasn't much of a challenge, since I'd found that most drugs failed to help my symptoms enough to justify the side effects, which seemed exaggerated in me as they did in many CFS patients I knew. On April 16, 1990, for no reason that I could figure out, I became violently ill—nausea, vomiting, diarrhea, intense muscle and joint pain, deep headache, a fever up from my now customary 97 to 103, cold sweats. It must have been a flu, although my overactive immune system usually spares me such illnesses. Apparently, before I fell into a frenzied sleep during the night, I'd scribbled a bedside note: Don't eat Vietnamese toilet paper rolls. Next morning, foremost in mind despite my condition was "I can't blow the Ampligen trial." So I took no ibuprofin, no Pepto Bismol, no Kaopectate. I lost ten pounds in the three days this attack took to pass.

When it was gone, I had a dream in which I was being hooked up to a machine lodged inside a side-by-side refrigerator. It had a digital readout that told my story: 238.

The technician said, "That's terrible, don't breathe."

I stopped breathing and the readout went to 0. As soon as I breathed, it rocketed to 238, which the technician kept saying was terrible. It seemed that the only way for me to be all right was not to breathe.

◆

AFTER THREE months of delays and two more months of screening procedures, I was notified that I'd been chosen to participate in the Ampligen field trial on July 23, 1990. I became *Patient 002*. Then there were two more months of delays and baseline data collection—the process by which our individual health pictures were established prior to being administered the drug or placebo, so that our progress in the trial could be measured. Baseline testing required that we walk to the point of collapse on an exercise treadmill. We did this on three separate occasions in order to measure how long it took before we collapsed and how our bodies responded throughout the physical challenge. After each test, we were bedridden for at least a week. Baseline also required a lengthy neurocognitive exam, which focused on all the things I could no longer do—puzzles, abstract reasoning, memory challenges—and a psychological exam and interview. There were chest x-rays, hours of extensive laboratory work that was lost and had to be redone, a lumbar puncture. I was given a pregnancy test.

Finally, I received my first infusion of either Ampligen or placebo on October 1, 1990, at 11:09 A.M. in the Solarium of the Clinical Research Center at Oregon Health Sciences University. The Research Center is housed in the oldest of OHSU's 27 buildings located on Marquam Hill, with a clear view of Mt. Hood and the Cascades to the west. The Solarium, in what used to be the maternity ward, is where new mothers once came to nurse their babies. I was sitting in a recliner, holding my daughter Becka's hand. It was eight months after I'd been invited to participate.

Ampligen. Quite helpfully, we were informed that it was a modified nucleotide, a small chain of chemicals known as a poly (I) poly (C 12 U) compound. It's a mismatched double-stranded RNA molecule that could cross the blood-brain barrier, which exists to protect the brain from bacteria and toxins in the bloodstream. A drug capable of both immunomodulatory and direct anti-viral effects, Ampligen sounded good enough to eat. But unfortunately it could neither be eaten nor injected, which of course I knew but now began to understand.

The drug was fragile, which was both good and bad. Good because it meant that my immune system wouldn't have time to form antibodies against Ampligen before it disappeared on its own. That meant its therapeutic properties would be maintained even at high doses. But Ampligen's fragility was bad because it meant that time was of the essence in getting it mixed and into the body; it had a short life and there was no flexibility in the schedule. It was going to be a challenge to be where I was required to be, at the time I was required to be there, several times a week. At least I didn't have to travel from out-of-town, like several other patients.

Then suppose I was getting the placebo? The word *placebo* is Latin for "I will please," of all things. Dr. Andrew Weil, in his book *Health and Healing*, notes that the word "entered English first as a Roman Catholic Church word designating a particular vesper service, came to mean 'flattery' and 'flatterer,' then found a home in the technical vocabulary of physicians. An 1811 edition of one medical dictionary identified it as 'an epithet given to any medicine adapted more to please than benefit the patient.'" As if that weren't bad enough, Norman Cousins in *Anatomy of an Illness* calls the placebo "an imitation medicine," and describes its use in testing new drugs this way: "Effects achieved by the preparation being tested are measured against those that follow the administration of a 'dummy drug' or placebo."

Listen to that language—flattery, fakery, a dummy drug. Anybody who responded to a placebo had to be a head-case. But on the other hand, as Dr. Arthur Shapiro wrote in the *American Journal of Psychotherapy*, "placebos can have profound effects on organic illness, including incurable malignancies." My own doctor had said that the placebo effect could amount to as much as a 30% improvement in symptoms. People respond to being cared for, even with salt water.

Oh boy. Here I am with an illness that too many people already suspect as being psychosomatic; what happens if I get better during the clinical trial and it turns out I've been getting the placebo? I'll be glad to be better, but humiliated by the implications (which will probably make me sick all over again).

How will I know?

This line of reasoning marks the path of placebomania that

every patient in a clinical field trial must travel. You become nutso, examining every scintilla of your body's reactions to everything. I developed a cough the other night; was that the drug working? My elbow hurts to the touch, so I've got to be on Ampligen. I fell asleep during the infusion; now tell me I'm not getting the drug!

◆

SINCE I was the only male among the eleven participants in Portland, someone christened us Floyd and the Ampligettes, like a fifties rock group. CFS strikes women far more frequently than men, at a rate estimated to be four to one. Our patient mix for the Ampligen trial in Portland was eleven to one. I kept wondering if our theme song would be something uplifting like "Could This Be Magic?" or something loony like "Witch Doctor."

I became an obsessed man. Ok, maybe I can't tell whether I'm on the drug or not. But was my fellow participant Lisa, a 29 year old former world-class racewalker and mother of three, getting the real or the dummy drug? I could—and did—watch her like Charles Darwin (who some researchers believe may have had CFS himself) watched the fauna on Albermarle.

Every Monday and Thursday morning at 10:00, we studied the plastic bottles in which the stuff came and peered at their yellow labels for clues. They were identical in every way. We studied ourselves and each other's every twitch, every fluctuation in temperature and blood pressure. I became jealous of her symptoms as she went through painful reactions to whatever she was getting. Did her legs really itch that much or was she imagining things? Looked like normal legs to me. Don't my legs itch just a little too? I began to talk with the other patients in the study; then with several from the three sites across the country: Charlotte, North Carolina; Houston, Texas; and Incline Village, Nevada. The other sites had started before us. They ought to know sooner how effective Ampligen was.

By Thanksgiving I was fairly certain and by Christmas I was positive. Salt water. I was getting placebo. I knew this the way I'm told a woman knows she's pregnant. In the very center of my self. Fine, Floyd, just hang in there. You'll get the drug in time.

For six months, enduring twice-a-week intravenous infusions and a third day's worth of tests, I waited for Phase One to end. We assumed that early April would be the ultimate 24 week target. But then additional patients began to participate as well, to start receiving infusions *three* times a week as though the trial had no real beginning or end dates and no set structure, so it was difficult to figure out when the first phase would actually conclude. We didn't worry. HEM had said it could last up to a year, and as fall ended and winter began I was prepared to go that long, despite being sure I was getting placebo, because I knew I'd get the drug in Phase Two. The veins in my arms were beginning to collapse, but there were veins in the hands or on the legs to use.

Then things changed.

On April Fool's Day, we were suddenly dismissed from the trial. Although the study was technically still in progress, and therefore the results were still "blinded," HEM had categorized some of us as Significant Responders and others as Nonresponders. How did they know, if they couldn't peek at the results? Nonresponders—which of course included those on placebo as well as those who had been receiving Ampligen but had only just begun responding to it—were told not to come back for infusions. No one knew what standards were used to determine significant response, but only two patients in Portland continued in the study. Since everyone was given the same dosage, regardless of body size or severity of illness, it seemed logical that people would respond at different rates. Why should they be punished for responding more slowly?

We were given no indication why the change in protocol had happened. We were given no indication of when the promised second phase would begin. Thanks, it was fun, see you around.

◆

IN THE MONTHS following this change, confusion and anger assaulted us like another virus. We were not the kind of patients able to swing into quick action, since most of us were bedridden by the combination of our illness and the rigors of the Ampligen trial. Why had HEM changed the rules? What could we do to get them to live up to their obligations and give us the drug as they promised? Should we sue? Was their problem economic and would legal action force them into bankruptcy? If it did, would this mean that Ampligen, which we had seen working on some of the participants, would not be available to the millions who needed it? Was their problem something other than economics—ethics, greed, some kink in the regulatory process that we hadn't been aware of? What were the doctors at each site saying? What was the FDA saying? Since the stress this had caused effected most patients' health, and since the removal of drug from patients who had begun to respond but were not classified as "significant responders" caused them to relapse dramatically, was HEM responsible for the costs of treatment just as they were responsible for my emergency medical costs associated with any problems that emerged as a direct result of our involvement in the study? Would they tell us what they'd learned about us from their lab work or follow our health situations in the interim? HEM was silent.

Of the 120 patients across the county who initially qualified for the clinical field trial, 92 had endured through April Fool's Day. The 92 of us tried to decide how to respond to the challenge of HEM's behavior. We asked a national CFS action group to help us because being both patients and advocates proved to be inefficient. We established links with successful AIDS patient advocates and with a few Congressmen. Litigation was filed by 18 patients in Federal District Court in Nevada seeking to force HEM to provide Ampligen as promised. Simultaneously fighting for our health, our contractual rights, and validity of our illness experience, we had to keep focused on the goal that had brought all of us into the study in the first place: getting an effective drug approved for use against CFS.

Meanwhile, at the annual conference of the American Society for Microbiology in Chicago, HEM released the findings of its clinical field trial. They were proclaiming the trial a great success: Ampligen was both safe and effective. Even the prestigious *Journal of the American Medical Association* carried the story.

By reading news reports and research summaries, we learned some things we already knew: Ampligen worked, it had some side effects, and those who, like me, were on placebo got worse over the course of the trial. Through reports and papers—rather than through word from HEM—we also learned some things we hadn't already known: the chaos in our immune systems was measurable and getting progressively worse if we weren't receiving Ampligen, we had anatomic holes in our brains that might or might not heal, without Ampligen we were deteriorating. They knew this and they let us go anyway, despite our contractual agreement.

According to their reports, HEM knew that "a significant number of placebo patients clinically deteriorate during the course of the clinical test," but failed to follow through with the promised drug. They knew that "more than two-thirds of the patients have extremely high and abnormal levels of natural immune fighting compounds, lymphokines and cytokines. Thus, we have gotten to the root of this disorder." Yet they denied us a drug to which we had been promised access, though their study of us had shown that "within a number of weeks these (Ampligen) patients get out of bed and begin to live a more normal life again." In regard to the holes in our brains, we "do not know whether the holes will heal, but we do know that with Ampligen there is a long-term recovery of certain memory functions." But they denied us the drug.

HEM applied to the FDA for approval of Ampligen for further testing. They continued giving it to some CFS patients who were not part of the clinical field trial, to some who were "significant responders," and to a scattering of AIDS patients under a separate field trial. But they denied it to the remaining members of our trial. In court, they were ordered to provide Ampligen to those who had sued, and they did so until the summer of 1993, when the last shipments of the drug were made to the clinical sites.

◆

How COULD something like this happen? Society has a need for experiments on sick patients to further biomedical science and conquer disease. As Hans Jonas of The New School of Social Research has noted, "the very destination of medical research, the conquest of disease, requires at the crucial stage trial and verification on precisely the sufferers from the disease." But society also is obligated to protect the human dignity and civil rights of individual patients, perhaps none more so than the seriously ill. The problem is how to control human experimentation adequately without closing off the possibilities of research on human subjects.

Regulation of medical research became a major public policy issue in America in the mid sixties. Wide-spread unethical practices among medical researchers were exposed in a 1966 *New England Journal of Medicine* article by Dr. Henry Beecher entitled "Ethics and Clinical Research." He described 22 examples of practices such as physicians feeding live hepatitis virus to patients in a state institution for the mentally retarded to study how the disease worked, or injecting live cancer cells into uninformed elderly and senile patients so that the body's immunological responses could be studied. Reform in the field of medical research then became a component of the overall civil rights movement.

I think people now believe that human experimentation is done ethically, safely and compassionately in this country. They believe that legal and regulatory safeguards protect those involved as subjects in medical research, that the law and government ensure abuses do not occur.

That's probably because medical research has not been written about from the subject's point of view. The other side—researchers, physicians, medical ethicists, philosophers, jurists, theologians, politicians—has been heard from. The view is different from inside rather than from beside the bed. I believe that my experience as a research subject is atypical, but it happened and can happen again.

Given the current drug approval process, even the best designed double-blind clinical trials have built-in ethical problems. An experimental treatment is being given to a group of patients though it may actually harm them; at the same time the treatment is being withheld from a similar group though it may actually help them. In the interests of medical science, patients who might have improved faster are denied that possibility by the clinical protocol. Sure, the patient consents to participate, but what real choice is there? The drug, with its wisp of hope, is often the only option for those who place their faith in traditional medical practice.

The paradox of this situation is clear: Randomized trials like the one I was involved with can never be reconciled with the best treatment for the individual patient participant because of random selection into experimental and control groups. But without such trials, physicians cannot know in advance what the best treatment for that particular patient actually is.

I hear that argument all the time. It doesn't wash. My experience suggests that in practice, neither clinical field trials nor their findings are as pure as their image might imply. One reason the drug DMSO has never been approved for general use is that blind studies cannot be conducted effectively because the drug produces a distinctive garlicky odor. Everyone knows who's getting DMSO. Instances of tampering with study results are common enough to appear in the news with sobering frequency.

It seems both more humane and more realistic—as well as more affordable than the current multi-step procedures—to enroll an adequate number of patients, give them all the experimental drug, and conduct ongoing studies using disinterested third parties to assess findings. It does not take an ethicist, a philosopher, or a physician to see what is wrong with the present way of approving new drugs in this country.

3

Trivia Tea

Baseball as Balm

QUESTION: Which 14 players have hit 30 or more home runs in a season in each league?

I'll give you the most recent one right off the bat. San Diego's Fred McGriff hit 31 homers in 1991, his first in the National league, after having hit over 30 the three previous seasons for the Toronto. I have ulterior motives in starting with McGriff, because he leads me to talk about a book called *The Answer Is Baseball*, by Luke Salisbury (Times Books, 1989).

Salisbury's book, as its subtitle proclaims, is a wonderful compendium "of questions that illuminate the great game." The questions it asks are "a door to the past and open the imagination," affording Salisbury the chance to examine issues that transcend baseball. One of the questions in the book is the same question posed here. At first I was annoyed to find my question already in print, having felt for years that I was the person who had thought it up. But then I was relieved to see that Salisbury had provided an incomplete answer. Excluding Fred McGriff, who hadn't yet hit his 30 for San Diego when the book was written, Salisbury didn't identify five players belonging on his list. This demonstrates yet another aspect of American culture for which poets must be responsible.

◆

I MUST confess at the outset that I use baseball as a form of alternative medicine. Its history and statistics are taken in like herbal remedies, its lore meditated on as a form of relaxation therapy, its long televised games approached as part of a natural healing process. Like a lot of natural healing, Harry Caray's voice and patter are extremely difficult to take, but I'm convinced now they do me good. However, it's worth mentioning that an herbalist once convinced me to take heaping tablespoons of something called Major Four, which was the precise consistency of sand, so I've already proven myself to be willing to try almost anything.

A lifelong active participant in the game, until my mid-thirties I was even one of those who dressed up twice a week in grotesque double knit uniforms to play slow-pitch softball under the lights at local parks. This is a direct progression from a childhood spent moving up from punchball to stickball to sandlot baseball, high school baseball and, finally, college baseball. But at 35, having discovered long-distance running, I found myself turning away from the old sport altogether. It was difficult learning to change my relationship to baseball; I had trouble finding new, more passive pleasures in it. But in the last few years, I've learned to tolerate its becoming a sport primarily read and thought about, an indoor sport despite my having grown up seeing games in person at Ebbets Field, Yankee Stadium, the Polo Grounds and Shea Stadium. The benefit is that this change has helped me cope with having a disabling and chronic disease.

A lifetime of baseball made me a numbers person. Stats are

facts. As of this writing, I've been sick for one thousand two hundred thirty four days.

In late fall of 1988, when I faced that hundred-mile-an-hour flu, I never imagined still being sick in the spring of 1992. Nothing is second nature to me anymore. I must think about every move. I could no more field a ground ball or hit a fastball than I could fly.

But I've learned to adjust. One way has been to reach into my past for baseball and, by redefining my relationship to it, open a path to the future. What worked with baseball has worked with other parts of my life as well.

✦

HAVING GROWN up in Brooklyn, NY, in the 1950s, I learned early to mark life's key moments according to what was happening in baseball. My family moved away from Brooklyn in the fall of 1957, exactly when the Dodgers moved away. The two events are inextricably linked in my mind. My father died in 1961, when I was 14, and those last months of his life are woven together with Roger Maris' pursuit of Babe Ruth's single-season home run record. I remember talking with my father during late summer and early fall about whether Maris had hit another that day, whether it would be Maris or Mickey Mantle to reach 60 homers first. My imagination was limited by my awe at his size, so I thought it would be the Mick. My father, stuck in history, didn't think either of them would do it. I actually got him to sit down and talk to me about this stuff. Unprecedented attention. One night he even came into my bedroom, picked up my bat from where it leaned against the door jamb, and showed me the famous Hack Wilson's batting stance. My father, his thick Havana cigar jutting from the corner of his mouth and reaching halfway to an imaginary first base, shifted his weight and I had to fight the impulse to duck. Those were the first real conversations we ever had, conversations in which he seemed to consider my opinions. Also the last. In the autumn of 1969, that zany season of the Miracle Mets when New York's infamous losers turned it around and won the World Series four games to one, I met the Irish poet Thomas Kinsella and first thought of myself as a writer.

So it isn't remarkable that I should return to baseball when I got sick. But it seems remarkable to me that I should find in it a way to help me adapt to being sick rather than another way to sadden me over my losses.

✦

I LOVE this question about 30 home run seasons because it can be reasoned out well enough that you almost feel in control. Approaching it is like approaching most questions about my health —one can understand enough about viruses and the immune system to formulate reasonable answers, even though they may not prove correct. It flexes the brain. It gives a sense of comprehension.

I also love it because in baseball, statistics offer the illusion of meaning. Early in my illness, when so much that was happening to me was undiagnosable, when questions about why my body was behaving as it was and how long it would continue were unanswerable, I developed a lust for facts. Viruses run from about 0.02 to 0.3 micrometers; a billion billion of them would fill one ping pong ball. DNA mixes four simple chemicals, like the repertoire of a good major league pitcher. The brain weighs about three pounds. Mine felt as though it was petrifying, the way decaying wood does as it turns to solid stone, and pressing me daily deeper into the bed.

Reason and facts, of course, aren't enough. Certain principles need to be set down before the question can be approached properly. One is that, unlike other major American sports, baseball is divided into two truly separate leagues with palpably different identities. Teams in the two leagues do not play one another during the regular season. Players might do well in the American league but fail utterly in the National. Catcher Lance Parrish comes to mind, an American league slugger who twice hit over 30 home runs for the Detroit Tigers but suffered through two miserable seasons with the National league's Philadelphia Phillies and is not a correct answer to the question. There are also historical principles. Nobody hit over thirty homers prior to 1920, when Babe Ruth hit 54. Keeping a clean, new baseball in play rather than using the same ball throughout the game had a lot to do with that, as did elimination of the spitball and other so-called trick pitches. More important for the question before us is that trading between leagues was uncommon until 1960. The only way a player could move from one league to the other was through waivers, a process by which any other team in his league might claim him before he could switch to the other league. Nobody who played before the sixties and was capable of hitting 30 home runs was likely to clear waivers, so there are no pre-sixties players among the 14 correct answers. Hank Greenberg came close, hitting 25 during his one National league season for the Pittsburgh Pirates after being sold to them for $75,000 by the Detroit Tigers in 1947 (the year I was born, which must explain my fascination with this question). Finally, there's the issue of what kind of player, still capable of hitting 30 home runs, would a team be willing to trade. Clumsy fielding power hitters, typically. Those first basemen or left fielders who are expendable because a team needs some real defensive help or pitching. Thus there are no shortstops or catchers on the list, no center fielders noted for their gloves. If those guys hit 30 home runs, teams keep them. Oddly enough, all but two of the 14 players on the list who were traded between leagues (four moved as free agents or were simply sold for cash) were traded for pitchers.

◆

ANSWERS FROM THE 1960's: Dick Stuart, Frank Robinson, Frank Howard.

The sixties was a decade of great home run hitters. It seems amazing to me that ten of the 13 lifetime home run leaders in the history of baseball were active in the sixties—sluggers such as Henry Aaron, Willie Mays, Harmon Killebrew, Reggie Jackson, Mickey Mantle, Ted Williams, Willie McCovey, Eddie Matthews and Ernie Banks. The all-time, single-season home run leader, Roger Maris, played in the sixties; he spent seven of those years in the American league and two in the National. Yet none of these great home run hitters had seasons of 30 or more in both leagues.

Only Dr. Strangeglove, Robbie and Hondo.

It's difficult to find a link between them. Lousy fielders? Frank Robinson, who—when not a designated hitter—played almost 90% of his games in the outfield, wasn't bad at all, with a lifetime fielding average of .984. His ex-teammate Paul Blair, who was considered a great fielder, had a lifetime fielding average only four thousandth of a percentage point better, .988, good enough to rank twelfth on the all-time list for outfielders. Slow runners? Robinson had several seasons in which he stole over 20 bases. They weren't all troublemakers, they weren't all losers (both Howard and Robinson appeared in World Series), and they weren't all flakes. If they shared something, maybe it was firsts: Robinson became baseball's first black manager, Howard was the first Ohio State University basketball player to play for the Dodgers, and Stuart was the first American player to become a star in Japan.

I picked up all these juicy tidbits looking through baseball books that friends brought as gifts. During the most acute phase of my illness, through the spring of 1989, I couldn't read anything. The last book I could read was a brilliant collection of short fiction called *The Riverside Stories* by my friend Andrea Carlisle. Then, all throughout the winter and spring of 1989, nothing. I remember that even *People Magazine* was too difficult to understand.

So I listened to music. I slept. In April, baseball began appearing on television. I could watch parts of games, dozing to the drone of Harry Caray's voice, waking for the fourth through sixth innings when he'd be replaced by Dwayne Staats, an announcer I could tolerate, and then dozing again to Harry's gravelly blabbering as the game ended.

Finally, in July, I was able to read David Halberstam's *Summer of '49*. Baseball had brought me back. At least, that's how it felt to me as I slowly emerged from the first phase of my illness. And reading Halberstam's book sent me into my earliest memories of baseball, the fifties and early sixties. I remembered being at Ebbets Field for a World Series game in which an outfielder fell into the stands trying to catch a ball. This, I was convinced, had to have been 1953, when I was seven. I don't think I can tell you how important it seemed for me to be able to find something this specific in my memory, which had grown so totally unreliable that I could neither place a close boyhood friend who had sent me a letter of good wishes nor remember my date of birth.

Ebbets Field. I remembered my father working the top off a miniature bottle of rye with his pocketknife between pitches, the Havana as always jutting from his mouth. I remembered seeing a pile of salted peanut shells sucked flat and dark under his slatted seat. He folded his scorecard like a funnel and his gravelly voice rose clear with the line drive's thock. I knelt on my seat beside him, cheering a split-second after he did.

After Halberstam's book, it wasn't long till I was leafing through *The Baseball Encyclopedia*, looking at its numbers the way I remembered seeing my mother leaf through magazines looking at the fashion photographs, not really absorbing anything, just feeling myself connected to something I valued, just passing time. I began to spend my two or three coherent hours a day at it. According to the World Series section of this 2,781 page treasure, and confirmed in Roger Kahn's great book *The Boys of Summer*, the game I saw was in 1952, not '53, and was in Yankee Stadium, not Ebbets Field. It was on October 5, Game #5, when Andy Pafko fell into the seats snaring Gene Woodling's drive to right off Carl Erskine, saving the Dodgers' 6-5 victory. Oh well, I was close.

On one of these idle summer leafings through The Book, I found myself gazing at Willie Mays' four inch chunk of numbers. In 1957, he'd done something that caught my attention—hit 26 doubles, 20 triples and 35 home runs. It took me almost three weeks of additional leafings to conclude that the only other modern players to hit more than 20 doubles, triples and home runs in one season were Jim Bottomley in 1928, Jeff Heath in 1941 and George Brett in 1979. Most who even came close—Kiki Cuyler, Lou Gehrig, Goose Goslin, Rogers Hornsby, Joe Medwick, John Mize, Stan Musial, George Sisler—are in the Hall of Fame or, in the case of Ryne Sandberg, likely to be. Another day, I focused on the listing for Frank Howard, who I remembered playing for the Dodgers after they had deserted me. Noticing that he'd hit over 40 home runs for the Washington Senators three times, I wondered if he'd ever hit that many for the Dodgers (31 was his tops). This was how my question got started.

I posed it to everybody I knew. Soon word got out that I could handle some light baseball reading. Also that I needed something other than the Encyclopedia, or else I'd drive them all nuts. My friends, many of whom had been steadfast for me during these months and yearning to offer something helpful, at last knew what they could bring for me.

◆

ANSWERS FROM THE 1970's: Dick Allen, Bobby Bonds, Reggie Smith, Jeff Burroughs.

The only one of these players mentioned in *The Answer Is*

Baseball was Reggie Smith. He hit 30 for the American league Red Sox in 1971 and 32 for the Dodgers in 1977. I don't want to brag or anything, but even sick, even with holes in my brain that show up on Magnetic Resonance Imaging tests, I remembered Allen and Bonds.

Nobody gets Burroughs. In a 16-year career, he hit 240 home runs, an average of just 15 per year. But he exploded in 1973, hitting 30 for the American league Texas Rangers, and again in 1977, hitting 41 for the National league Atlanta Braves in their friendly stadium. That's almost a third of his lifetime home runs in two seasons. Despite having won an American league Most Valuable Player award (only Frank Robinson and Dick Allen from the list were also MVPs) and despite his two explosive home run seasons, it turns out that Burroughs wasn't a memorable player.

A quick look at the list from the seventies suggests that players this productive who still get traded probably do so because they're, er, difficult people. Allen was traded four times between 1970 and 1975. Bonds played for eight teams in his 14-year career and Burroughs with five. Smith was widely regarded as a moody, troublesome player and was with four different teams between 1973 and 1982. Hell, if they played in the nineties instead of the seventies, they'd be zillionaires, compounding their fortunes with each move between teams.

Thinking about Dick Allen makes me consider how fragile the human body is and how whimsical the fortune that holds it intact. Even the powerful body of someone capable of hitting 351 major league homers, which places him among the fifty greatest sluggers in the game's history. In 1966, still a sprightly 24-year old, Allen dislocated his shoulder while sliding and missed two dozen games (still hitting 40 home runs). His next season ended in late August when his right hand broke through the headlight of an old car he was pushing. In 1968 he had a groin injury and missed ten games; two years later he missed 40 games with an Achilles tendon injury and various pulled muscles. In 1973, Mike

Epstein, who was larger than Allen and known affectionately as Superjew, stepped on his leg after Allen dove for an bad throw, breaking a bone. He missed more than half the season. Although he hit 32 home runs in 1974, Allen missed 34 games with a sore shoulder and bad back. He retired in 1977, at 35, after spending most of the previous two seasons on the disabled list.

Not only are bodies essentially frail, they're part of a system. It's so easy for athletes to think of their bodies as either separate from their essential selves—a kind of machine—or at the other end of the scale, as their entire selves. At 41, my body was in its best shape ever and I was dangerously close to seeing it as invincible. Running 45-50 miles a week, winning ribbons for races at anywhere between a mile and a marathon, I was convinced—had proof—that the older I got the better I got. I weighed less than when I was in junior high school and my percentage of body fat was under twelve. The more I pushed myself, the stronger I seemed to get. Now I understand that the kind of rigorous exercise I thrived on actually weakens the body, rendering it vulnerable to viral attack. Stress compromises the immune system. According to an August 1991 article in *the New England Journal of Medicine*, "stress is associated with the suppression of a general resistance process in the host, leaving persons susceptible to multiple infectious agents." While I don't believe I made myself sick by overexercising and failing to heed my levels of stress, I didn't do anything to help myself either. My body reminded me that it is part of an integrated system, neither more nor less than my self. I've been on the Disabled List since December 7, 1988.

✦

THERE ARE several players you'd swear had 30 home run seasons in each league. People mention Orlando Cepeda among the first half dozen names, remembering his one season (1973) swinging for Boston's Green Monster in left field. But he only hit 20 homers that year. Tony Perez actually came closer than Cepeda, hitting 25 homers for Boston in 1980, but few people whom I've asked this question remember Perez playing in Fenway. Lee May hit over 30 for three straight years with the National league's Reds, but never more than 27 for Baltimore in the American league. Bobby Murcer came as close, topping 30 for the Yankees, then hitting 27 for the National league's Cubs. Although it's difficult to remember he was ever this productive, Joe Pepitone hit 31 for the Yankees in 1966 and four years later hit 26 in a National league season split between the Astros and Cubs. Joe Carter, who has hit over 30 five times in the American league, hit but 24 for the San Diego Padres in 1990. Johnny Mize and Roy Sievers were sluggers who had passed their heydays just before interleague trading began; Graig Nettles, Rusty Staub and Ken Singleton are among recently retired almosts. George Foster, whose 52 home runs for the National league Giants in 1977 were the most for any player in that league between 1949 and now, only played 15 games in the American league, the final games of his 18-year career. Kirk Gibson, surprisingly enough, never hit 30 anywhere.

At the end of 1991, there were still a few active players with good chances to join the list, but they each fell short. Jack Clark kept coming the closest of anyone in history, having hit 35 in 1987 for the National league's Cardinals despite playing in mammoth Busch Stadium and having hit 28 in 1991 for the Red Sox. He also hit 27 for the Yankees in 1988. But in 1992, he hit only five and was finished with baseball. Eddie Murray, who hit over 30 homers five times for Baltimore in the American league, had topped out at 26 for the Dodgers. He hit 27 for the Mets in 1992, but then returned to the American league to continue his illustrious career. I was thrilled when the Seattle Mariners acquired Kevin Mitchell from the Giants in 1991, figuring that if he stayed healthy, he ought to hit 65 in the Kingdome to go with his two National league seasons of more than 30, or at least join Darrell

Evans as the only players to hit 40 in both leagues. But he hit only nine in his one American league season, then went back to the National League to hit 30 again for the Reds in 1993 before heading to Japan. Now, barring trades or the miraculous restoration of Darryl Strawberry as a New York Yankee, there do not seem to be any candidates for the list.

Then there was Nick Esasky. Esasky hit 30 homers for the Red Sox in 1990 before signing with Atlanta in the National League for the 1991 season. But then he was stopped at the peak of his career by a mysterious disease spookily similar to my own.

Esasky had come home. He'd signed a three-year, $5.7 million contract with the Braves that would let him play just a half hour from his suburban home in Marietta, where he'd lived for years with his wife and children. In March of 1991, one week into spring training, came the weakness and severe fatigue.

"At first I thought it was the flu and that it would go away," he told *People Magazine*. "Then I began to get headaches and nausea, and I felt light-headed and dizzy."

Esasky saw more than 30 specialists in the first six months without a definitive diagnosis. Ballplayers do everything big; I only saw a dozen specialists in my first six months. Diagnosed only after he'd reached the point of not caring what to call his illness, the problem was damage to Esasky's inner ear caused by a viral infection. I have Chronic Fatigue Syndrome as a remnant of my viral infection. Esasky has vertigo as the remnant of his. It's chilling to imagine what it must have felt like for him to face a major league curve ball, or catch a hard throw at first base. Actually, he put it well, telling *Sports Illustrated* that "it felt like I was in slow motion, and everything else was moving very quickly around me." When I tried to run after my illness began, I'd lost the ability to gauge my speed or direction and fell off the margin of the wooded trail I was on, rolling 15 feet downhill before coming to rest against the trunk of an old-growth red cedar.

Esasky also told *Sports Illustrated* about his quest for cure. An orthodontist removed his braces. He took infusions of antibiotics for Lyme Disease, which he didn't have. An allergist tested him, a psychologist talked with him and a hypnotist tried "to see if we could just block it out by mind power. That didn't work. Hocus-pocus doesn't do it."

Well, no. Neither did eating sand. In late 1991, Esasky was working with a neurologist who directs the Dizziness and Balance Center in Wilmette, Illinois, retraining his balance system. He was trying to overcome vertigo by learning how to not feel sick whenever he moved, hoping eventually to play again for the Braves. But he can accept if it never happens.

"Either way," he says, "I will be taken care of. This has taught me that there are a lot of people out there with problems much worse than mine."

Sounds like jock-speak, the sort of innocuous thing players say to reporters all the time, an out-take from *Bull Durham.* Except I believe him. I used to think baseball was what connected me to these guys. Now, when I get the urge to heft my hand-carved co-cobolo cane and cock it like a bat, I do it in honor of Nick Esasky's comeback attempt.

✦

ANSWERS FROM THE 1980's: Jason Thompson, Dave Winfield, Greg Luzinski, Dave Kingman, Darrell Evans, Larry Parrish.

In *The Answer Is Baseball,* Luke Salisbury left out the last three of these players, even Evans, the only player with 40 in both leagues. Kingman is going to have the distinction of being the one player among the 20 greatest home runs hitters in baseball history *not* to be elected to the Hall of Fame. He was traded so often—shuttling from league to league, once even playing for four different teams in one season—and did virtually nothing but hit home runs and strike out, that it's hard to miss him as a candidate for this list. Missing Larry Parrish I can understand; he can be confused with Lance Parrish, who as I said before is the Parrish you'd think ought to be on this list and isn't.

It's hard to be intimate with 1980's baseball. This was the era of escalating salaries, strikes and lockouts, of what Roger Angell, writing in *The New Yorker*, called an "omnipresent industry, with its own economics and politics and crushing public relations." Television coverage made fans familiar with teams throughout the league—the Cubs and Braves on giant cable stations, other teams through the saturation coverage provided by ESPN—even as familiarity with one's local team became prohibitively expensive or their locations inaccessible.

Angell also says "American men don't think about baseball as much as they used to, but such thoughts once went deep." He's probably right, and I realize that my own situation is unusual in that I have so much time in which I am at home, unable to function well, and freed—in a sense—to think about baseball. I feel lucky still to have thoughts about it that run deep because I think baseball has given me hope. It links my past, which damage to my brain threatened to pillage, with a present that I live in largely outside of time. The flow of my days, the accumulation of my weeks and months, is simply not like most people's anymore. I often spend two-thirds or more of my time in bed and am disconnected from time in a way most people aren't—it only matters what time it is when I have to see my doctor or eat lunch with a friend or watch a ballgame or call the editor of *The Gettysburg Review* to ask for two more weeks to finish this essay. Baseball also links my past and present with an uncertain future. I don't know how long my illness will last or where it will take me, but can Will Clark relocate his power stroke and hit 30 home runs this year for the Texas Rangers to join my list?

Don't get me wrong, this isn't all I have to live for. I have love, family, friends, writing. But it's an important and satisfying way for me to feel coherent in a world suddenly very different than I thought it would be. Baseball moves me again.

◆

IT WAS the autumn of worst to best. The Atlanta Braves and Minnesota Twins, both last-place teams in 1990, were challenging for the pennant in 1991. It seemed as though anything was possible. The Soviet Union was breaking apart. I'd been given a one month writer's residency at Centrum, an arts organization on the grounds of Fort Worden State Park in Port Townsend, Washington.

Near the end of September, my friend Eric drove up from Portland to take me on the one trip I was willing to make away from the gorgeous isolation of Centrum. We went by car and ferry to the Kingdome, where the Seattle Mariners were hosting the Texas Rangers and Nolan Ryan would pitch. Indoor baseball, the apotheosis of my redefined relationship to the sport.

I'd been to the Kingdome before, in 1977. That visit was to bring my nine year old son to see his first major league game. It took me nine years to get him to a game because 1977 was the first time a team played close enough to where we lived to make the trip viable. As soon as we walked into the stadium I knew it would be hard to forgive myself—Matt, forget what you're seeing, this isn't a baseball park. It was Picture Day, we were right down on the carpet snapping pictures of such luminaries as Craig Reynolds and Ruppert Jones, hearing a kind of recirculated fan noise that could only be described as otherworldly.

We didn't go back to the Kingdome. Fortunately, at least in terms of the family's baseball continuity, we moved to the midwest for a while, close enough to St. Louis so that I could make amends.

Yet in September of 1991, I was delighted to be entering the Kingdome again. Nolan Ryan is six months older than I am. I think I planned to wave my cane at him and yell that he should pitch till he's fifty. Maybe I just planned to pay my respects to a great performer, or see what he really looks like in his body the same age as mine, how his competitive spirit and drive manifest themselves without burning him up. I don't know.

We got there early enough to watch Ryan warm up. The Mariners' pitcher, Rich DeLucia, was two years old when Nolan Ryan began his major league career for the Mets in 1966. DeLucia came out onto the carpet just after Ryan, appearing to serious cheering from the crowd, began his slow walk toward the bullpen in left field. DeLucia immediately started throwing from the bullpen mound in right, his pitches snappy enough to hear. He was all business; I watched him for a while because Ryan was taking so long to make his way out. When I looked back, Ryan was sitting on the carpet stretching his legs. By the time DeLucia was through with his warmups, Ryan was finishing his stretches. Then he sashayed toward the left field wall and began casually flipping a ball toward the infield, where his catcher was standing. His motion was like an outfielder's after catching a lazy fly ball with no one on base—a few trotting steps, a toss that used a minimum of arm and maximum of leg and upper body. It was twenty minutes before he approached the bullpen mound and began pitching, easy at first, not hard enough to pop the catcher's mitt until several more minutes had passed. The man was careful with his body.

Our seats were directly behind home plate. Peering through the chain-link safety screen took some getting used to, but by game time I was set. When the Mariners came up to hit in the bottom of the first, I felt both excited and nervous, as though perhaps I'd have to hit against Ryan later in the game. I remember thinking, where did that come from? And thank you, baseball, for giving it to me again.

What remains with me most clearly is the grunting sound Ryan made as he delivered a fastball. There would be this 'uhhhh,' almost but not quite simultaneous with the sound of the ball hitting Ivan Rodriguez's glove. I don't imagine Ryan worried too much about tipping off his fastball with the noise, which he didn't make on curves or changeups.

He'd already won 29 games and struck out 493 batters—9% of both lifetime totals—by the time his young catcher was born in the late autumn of 1971. Jeez, I love doing these numbers. Did he really let the kid call his pitches? Seemed to. Would he sit with him between innings to discuss strategy? No, he went into the clubhouse between most innings. Probably to work out on the stationary bike.

This was a late-season game, meaningless in the standings, and I wondered if Ryan would coast through five innings to get his victory and then leave. He didn't, bless his heart. I got to see him strike out ten batters through eight innings and win the 314th game of his career, tying him with Gaylord Perry for 14th on the all-time victory list. I got to see him bear down against the Mariners' fine young star, Ken Griffey, Jr., pitching to him with obviously greater intensity than he pitched to Omar Vizquel, who was hitting .230, or Dave Valle at .194. Before his second appearance against Ryan, I got to watch Griffey in the on-deck circle, which was about twenty feet from where I sat. The kid looked different than before his first appearance, when I noticed him scanning the seats behind home plate to check out the young women in their Indian summer finery.

It felt wonderful to be where I was, in the Seattle Kingdome late on a Wednesday afternoon in September, watching indoor baseball, letting numbers run through my head, telling Eric about games I'd seen as a boy, listening to his tales of watching Roberto Clemente and Bill Mazeroski play at Forbes Field in Pittsburgh. We didn't eat hot dogs because I have to be very careful about chemicals in my food, but we'd brought apples. There's always a new way to see things.

PART TWO

Turning Inward

"The pale inner left arm pierced and withdrawn.
A sweat-heated pillow flattened under my neck,
    I lay and fingered my mental parts.

A draft stirred the red curtain: a figure
at the foot of the bed, observing like a brother.
    Not much trace of him before our trouble.

But I needed nothing there. They must be letting
anybody in. I lifted a ham
    in thoughtful ease. The curtain settled back.

My tablets, bitten to a flour,
melted in an aftertaste of coffee.
    Awareness turned inward: a memory echoing,

with the blood beating injected in the face . . ."

                —Thomas Kinsella, from "Visiting Hour"

4

Running Down

YEARS HAVE passed, patience has been exercised, but my body still doesn't work right. Though I have no reason to believe it ever will again, I keep checking.

I stretch in the mornings. I try to walk outside every day, "pushing the envelope" as the old flyboys used to say, finding out if I can go for twenty minutes today instead of the eighteen I did yesterday. There are months when I can't walk for exercise at all, but then, slowly, I begin again. Head-high weeds will have grown over a path I follow through the fields around my house. The wire fence which deer leaped in fleeing from me early one morning might be entirely hidden by grass and the sagging wooden gate will have fallen altogether. It seems like a new world and my walks become outer as well as inner explorations. About once a year, and against my doctors advice, I experiment with a regimen of situps and pushups. In the old days, I would do a quick fifty or seventy-five of each after running ten miles, but now I am exhausted before I can work long enough to be sore the next day. Some spring days, I pick up a small rock or a pine cone, toss it in the air, and swing my cane at it like a bat. Old habits die hard.

Not long ago, when my body felt infused with capacity, I knew that I had Power. There was a deep confidence that came with this knowledge, a sense of my body solid in space, a sense that there was little I could not do. I'm a very small man, barely 5′4″ on a good day, and this sense of capacity, which had been slow to evolve, felt somehow vital to my way of being in the world. At 41, I was running faster than ever before. I loved to wear tight tee shirts, size small, just a bit too snug across the shoulders and chest. *Pull down thy vanity, I say pull down!*, old Ezra Pound chanted in *Canto LXXXI*. Indeed, before I turned 42, the Power had vanished. I couldn't run a block. Run, hell, I couldn't always be sure I'd make it upstairs to the bathroom without having to lie on the landing. I moved like Walter Brennan rather than Alberto Salazar.

Of course I look back. I wonder how I got sick, if it was something I did to myself, something I could have avoided. I find myself fantasizing that by fully comprehending how it happened, I could devise a way to reverse the steps and cure myself. Now when I hear the sputtering Volkswagen Bug that announces my mail has arrived at the end of the driveway, I'm often tempted to run the hundred yards up there to see what's come. I can't—I'd be bedridden for a week. So I walk up slowly and think about running, about the glory days. I can actually feel, as though it has been embedded in my body through some para-sensory memory, what it was like to turn the corner in Lake Oswego's George Rogers Park and cross the bridge to the finish line at the end of my favorite 10K race. I can remember running alongside the same half-dozen runners in almost every race, people I didn't know but who ran at the same pace I ran, people whose way of breathing or of holding their arms were as familiar to me as my own son's. Recently, one of those runners showed up for a reading I gave at a local bookstore. When I saw him, it was all I could do to keep from crying. He looked younger than he had the last time I saw him, which was as I breezed past him in the final hundred yards of a 10K race, and at 47 he was even thinner than he was at 42.

"I wondered," he said, "if you would read any poems about running."

One thing that chronic, long-term illness gives you is plenty of time to think. It's amazing to me how much of a sick person's thinking is about the body; not just about its symptoms and their daily changes, every little ache, every new mark, but what the body has accomplished, what it has been able to do when pushed. It's a kind of hopefulness, I think. If I can re-experience what it felt like to push through my body's limits and finish that marathon when I ran much too fast for the first twenty miles, or to break that 38 minute barrier in a 10K, or to score that impossible touchdown in high school when I ran fifty-four yards with an invisible shield between me and all those tacklers, then maybe I can challenge it again to push through this latest limit.

Illness also changes the way you dream. Because sleep disturbance is a hallmark of Chronic Fatigue Syndrome, for years I have seldom managed to sink into dream sleep. However, when I do, the dreams are often like nothing I have dreamt before. And not all of them are bad dreams, such as the rotten celery or the side-by-side refrigerator dreams. I've flown several times, even managing to learn how to turn over in flight so that I could look down at the ground. I've hit home runs and run in the woods so fast that the trees were a verdant blur. But most often, I am lost in fog.

✦

There it is at last, a green sandwich-board sign on the shoulder of the road that must be the first mile marker. With dreamy ambiguity, I think: It's about time. The number 1 is huge; then I'm close enough to see that the word below it is Year.

I WOULD never have dreamed this. Time has turned inside-out for me. Days trudge along as though depleted by the effort of sunrise. Then suddenly a week has passed, and soon a month, and then one full year has simply gone. Thinking back, sometimes it feels like one long day; other times it feels like a whole decade.

Me? Mr. Energy himself, with the full-time job, the second career as a poet and prose writer, the runner with a corkboard of ribbons on the wall, the devoted father, the lover? No way. But now, all of a sudden, I can't do what I never had to think about doing. Nevermind the daily six miles, what about *can I walk to the corner?* When I can't work anymore because I can't concentrate, can't add or spell, can't remember, CAN'T THINK, I must wonder if it's even me anymore.

✦

This has to be the last turn. The road is straight again and I'm running all alone. I look up, but there is no colorful banner arcing across the road, no clock to read, nobody alongside cheering. I raise my arm to check the time, to be sure I haven't miscalculated, but my watch face is blank and so I look ahead again. It's true. There's no finish line.

I only know one thing to do. All my years of running tell me this: relax, dig down, keep going.

✦

HOW DID I get sick? After years of telling my story to doctors and friends and fellow patients, after going over it endlessly, I still have questions. It still seems to matter.

In the spring of 1988, I was "the picture of health." The summer before, when I was president of the Portland Poetry Festival,

I hosted a dinner during the annual four-day series of readings, which was attended by most of the writers invited from around the country. I remember one of them, the brilliant Oakland-area poet and novelist Diana O'Hehir, asking why I was eating so little of the food I had prepared.

"I have to watch my weight," I said. "I've got a race next weekend."

She blinked and put down her fork. "Why, you don't have an ounce of fat on you. Eat, for God's sake. This is a celebration of richness."

Missing the explicit, though gentle, chastisement, I was thrilled to hear her say I hadn't an ounce of fat on my body. Good, I thought, that's certainly the goal. Perhaps I really was nuts, but I sure was fit.

Starting in mid-June with Portland's Cascade Run Off, I won age group ribbons in at least one race every month, regardless of the distance. During one week, I ran in a one-mile race on Thursday, a 10K on Saturday and an 8K on Sunday. My son and I took third place in the Father/Son category of the Portland Marathon's five-miler, fulfilling a long-standing dream of competing together. Soon thereafter, an entry in my running diary says simply "Not well."

Looking back at the diary now, I try to pinpoint the first signs. The notes tell me a lot more now than they did then. There was a nagging problem with one hamstring from April on, a feeling of weakness in the other hip, nothing to worry about. On June 9, there is an entry saying "have a cold" on a day I ran seven miles at 6:00 A.M.

It was just a cold. I ran through it.

On June 21 is the first of what will soon be regular entries that say "bad, interrupted sleep." On July 18, since I couldn't sleep I ran seven miles at 5:30 A.M.

Ok, so I ignored a few potential signs of trouble, slight indicators that things weren't right. Who doesn't?

At the end of July, I went on a business trip to New York.

Since I would be travelling all day Wednesday, I thought it good to run a few extra miles Monday ("Poor sleep, tired") and Tuesday ("Had to run after work because couldn't wake up"). In New York on Thursday, I ran nine miles through Central Park at 6:10 A.M. Eastern Time. That was a July of New York's most horrible heat and humidity; I ran in it all three days, at three in the morning body-time, not having run in 90 degree/90 percent weather for years.

In August, my friend Jim Kaufmann visited from Illinois. He was preparing for a fall marathon in Chicago, so I ran with him for nine days, jacking my weekly mileage up a sudden 20% despite bad sleep and continued feelings of fatigue. What the hell, I was racing so well I couldn't be sick or anything.

September 15: "wish I wasn't so tired." Later that month, I forgot to put my contact lenses in for the Portland Marathon five-miler, so ran it blind. I began a trend of being unable to wake up in time for races, five times getting to the starting line just as the gun went off. Still, I raced. I trained a little harder to get myself through this "bad patch."

It never really went away. Then came my trip to Washington, D.C., in December, when I got hit with the flu—or whatever it was—that six months of this behavior had been inviting. In retrospect, I am astonished by the fact that I forced myself to run two loops of the Mall despite how ill I was. Though I couldn't walk to the bookstore I'd been looking forward to visiting, couldn't bring myself to eat the Indian dinner I'd planned to enjoy for months ahead of time, couldn't even look at the big snifter of cognac I ordered in the hotel bar to help me sleep, I ran. The next morning too, through sleet and a harsh Washington wind, over to the Vietnam Veterans' Memorial for a visit I'd promised myself to make.

Even after the way I felt in Washington, I came home and kept running for a few weeks. My symptoms kept getting worse, magnifying geometrically as I kept running, kept trying to see myself through it. Finally, when moving through the air felt like moving through water, when I could still breathe but felt like I was being sucked down to my death, I decided I needed help.

For most of us who have been running a long time, this probably isn't an unusual string of behaviors—which could be a problem.

I don't believe that I made myself sick. CFS has a cause, an agent, which will most probably turn out to be a virus—was it that June cold I had? Was it something I caught on the plane to Washington, my immune system weakened by what I was doing to myself? This isn't something I deserved, nor is it punishment for pushing myself too hard. As Susan Sontag would say, it's not a metaphor.

I didn't hit the wall.

But I do believe that I did nothing to help myself and everything to hurt myself by not listening to my body. Oh, I heard my body—the hamstring and hip, the tiredness. But I didn't listen.

✦

IN DECEMBER of 1988, acknowledging that I was finally at a complete collapse, I entered the medical maze. It was like wandering through the Mother of All Finishers' Chutes. Thinking the worst was over, that here at last I would get taken care of, I found instead chaos. Continue along the channel, please; don't pass the person in front of you; give us your number; don't ask us for your results, we'll let you know. Initial tests revealed that several organs were malfunctioning—liver, thyroid, possibly brain, but nothing was conclusive. I stopped taking niacin, which had been prescribed to control my genetic cholesterol problems, but my liver didn't clear up. For months, as I continued to get worse, I was shuttled from specialist to specialist. When I finally got to the right doctor, I knew at once. His office is at the top of the long, hard hill on the Cascade Run-Off course.

✦

It seems as though I've been leaning into this hill for miles, using my whole body to work the climb, keeping my eyes dead ahead. My form is still all right, but I don't know how much longer I can keep it that way.

So I imagine the road levelling off. I imagine a long, deep breath, a straight back and my arms loosening up again. I imagine chancing a quick glance at what lies ahead and see a slight dip in the road that I believe means the rest of the way will be mostly downhill.

I imagine it and by imagining it, I command the moment to come that much sooner.

5

The Roosevelt Chair

I WAS MAKING notes as I sat in my recliner. From December 1988 through January 1992, when I filled an hour in thinking about this, I probably spent an average of three to four hours a day in my recliner. Conservatively estimating, since there were many more eight-hour days than one-hour days, let's go with three hours a day for three years and 24 days. Ok, 1,119 days at three hours each means I spent 3,357 hours in my recliner, or nearly 140 full days. A lot of chair time, which lead me to consider the recliner as the Most Important Chair in my life, replacing, at long last, the Roosevelt Chair.

✦

IN MY boyhood home, we had a fancy chair no one sat in sequestered by the fireplace no one lit. It was a crown-topped, button-backed Hitchcock chair that came from Franklin Delano Roosevelt's summer house at Campobello.

My mother bought the chair at an auction in 1957, the year we moved from Brooklyn to a small island off Long Island's south shore. The Roosevelts were selling personal items to raise money for polio research. Although Jonas Salk's killed-virus vaccine had been approved for use two years earlier, there was controversy over its long-term effectiveness. Research into an oral attenuated-virus vaccine was still going on and funds were needed.

I had been a Polio Pioneer in 1954, lining up with my class-mates for vaccination in the gym at Public School #235, my first encounter with human medical experimentation. Everything had been explained to me, the great value and importance of what was about to occur, but I couldn't get out of my mind the idea that I was going to get a shot even though I wasn't sick. A typi-cal adult trick. I remember becoming invisible, as only a child with my background can, then wandering out of line at the cru-cial moment. Soon I was approached by the nurse, who was also my friend Douglas' mother, and asked a simple question.

"Did you get stuck yet?"

Just what I needed to hear. Nodding vigorously, fighting back tears, I watched her slap a band-aid across my left arm. It was that easy.

About an hour later, the principal came into our room and beckoned to the teacher. There was something in his right hand, a small vial perhaps, though I was sure it must be the needle meant for me. He looked unhappy, as though he might have to endure the extra injection himself if he couldn't locate the unac-counted-for second grader.

"Did anyone here miss his vaccination?" my teacher called from the door. *His.* They know it's me. I sat on my hands, liter-ally, and looked around the room like everyone else.

Nothing bad happened as a result. I couldn't believe it. Nor-mally, for perpetrating the least mischief at school, I would be punished extraordinarily at home. No dinner, no playing with friends for two weeks, no listening to records until my next report card. But I got away with the Polio Caper completely.

Until the following summer, when our neighbor's teenaged son contracted polio. I remember my parents' hushed voices at the dinner table and their great relief that I had been vaccinated. I couldn't sleep that night. By morning, I had confessed.

We all went to the doctor's office the next day for gamma globulin shots. I was made to watch as first my father, then my brother bared their buttocks for injections. My brother, because of his size, had to endure the unscrewing of one syringe and screwing on of a second. I can still see the stubby needle top protruding above his skin.

✦

MY MOTHER is a former torch singer who once had her own radio show on WBNX in the Bronx. She was broadcast opposite Rudy Valee and loved to say that no one, not even her own parents, listened to her show.

She also loved to say that she got the Roosevelt chair for a song. It appeared in our house one winter afternoon, shortly after we had moved. My father sauntered over to it when he got home from work, studied it while fitting a cigar into his brown plastic holder, and never said a word about the chair as far as I can remember.

There was a disc stuck low in its back that bore the number 75. Tucked away in a drawer of her chiffonier, my mother had a booklet which proved to any doubters that item #75, desk chair, was from the estate of Franklin Delano Roosevelt. When someone new came to visit, my mother would send me to fetch the booklet. I never minded. She kept it beside her stash of licorice twists and if company was there, she would never bawl me out for taking one.

I sometimes think of that part of my childhood as The Licorice Wars. Licorice twists, black Dots, chocolate flavored licorice ropes, Nibs. She would buy packages of licorice to set out in her various bowls, dishes and jars, always ordering me to leave them alone. But I loved licorice and simply could not obey her, a fact that she certainly understood. My approach was to raid her supplies equally—one from each container, a few from each hiding place—so as not to tip her off. Of course, she always knew when I'd staged an assault because, I was sure, she counted the stores late at night after I'd gone to sleep. Raided licorice cost me countless hours of lost television, of afternoons indoors instead of playing ball with my friends, of evenings when no one in the house would talk to me. Curiously, my mother didn't particularly like licorice herself; chocolate was her passion. And when she bought a kind of licorice that I didn't care for, like those raspberry flavored mutations, she'd throw them away and never buy them again. Who was the licorice for? My father was diabetic and I never saw a guest take any (believe me, I watched). I would guess they were not for anyone so much as for the War effort.

✦

WHEN THE chair first arrived, its cane seat sagged where the President had sat. I imagined him writing at his desk up there at Campobello Island, dressed in a dark suit even though it was August, a cigarette in its holder clamped between his teeth. He would look up from the paper, his jaw jutting cloudward, to seek inspiration by gazing at the gorgeous Bay of Fundy dotted with all those other little islands. This was a place he had come to since he was a child, since he was my age. I could see myself there, waiting to swim with him in the cold water. Our faces, Franklin's and mine, were drenched because of the summer heat, but he would be done with his work soon.

I examined every detail of the chair. Its lavish arms were scarred by ash. The seat front was nicked, I assumed, by his braces. Its black paint was badly faded. From across the room, it seemed twisted slightly to the left, as though looking for the door.

My mother couldn't stand it. If the chair was going to be in her living room, the chair was going to look right!

She had it tightened to a timeless silence. She painted it over in deep black, covering the wreaths of golden flowers that had twined up its limbs. She decorated it with stripes instead. A black leather cushion was glued to the chair back. Another was placed on the seat, its tassels dangling to the floor.

The tapered legs, turned in a dozen rings, were hidden from the window's light when she placed the chair near the fireplace. Daily, she swept dust from the fireplace floor with a broom intended for ashes.

I always imagined that area of the living room as cordoned off, existing behind velvet ropes strung from the piano to the patio door. Of course, there are lessons in this, as there are lessons in the unlit fireplace—that ours was a house in which life was arrayed rather than lived, that I was a boy who would never try to sit in the Roosevelt chair, that my mother would retouch a Picasso if its colors didn't go with her living room.

✦

AFTER MY father died, in 1961, and after my mother had mourned for him a year or more, she began to go on cruises. Not having worked in the twenty-three years of her marriage, never having been trained in any profession, long ago having given up her singing and costume-design careers, she was virtually unable to support us until an old friend from Brooklyn hired her to be a travel agent.

She had once been to Belgium, in 1928, and had read the first two of Balzac's *Droll Stories*, so she felt quite comfortable booking clients to Europe. She wasn't sure where Portugal was in relation to Luxembourg, but nobody went to Luxembourg anyway.

They went to Switzerland, if she had anything to say about it, and she certainly knew where Switzerland was, especially its gorgeous beaches. It was close to Belgium, where she herself had been, after all. Soon she was availing herself of the travel agent's primary perk, free travel. Afraid to fly, she took to the seas. She would be gone for two, sometimes four weeks at a time, leaving me with grocery money and instructions on how to behave in her absence.

No parties. No more than one friend at a time in the house. No using the oven (I became a fifteen-year-old expert on sauté cooking). Stay out of the licorice. Do your homework. Don't sit in the Roosevelt chair.

I used to think the most seductive thing I could offer a girl who visited my home was the chance to sit in the Roosevelt chair. Oddly enough, few of them went wild over the experience. Since I was essentially a good boy, despite my involvement in the Polio Caper, and since I was tied up playing high school football or baseball, I obeyed the rules to a humiliating degree. But I couldn't keep myself, or my one visitor at a time, out of the Roosevelt chair. Alone as it was beside the cold fireplace, ill-lit, tight, it was an awful place to do homework. It was an awful place in which to read my sports magazines. An awful place to try and kiss somebody. That was the theater in which I operated.

◆

THOMAS KINSELLA has written extensively about leaving home, about departure and change. His great poem "Phoenix Park," set in Dublin in the late sixties, begins: "One stays or leaves. The one who returns is not / The one, etcetera. And we are leaving."

Two simple options. You stay home or you go away. However, since to leave is to change oneself in fundamental ways, knowing how to choose is anything but simple. At eighteen, based primarily on the life I had lived at home, and secondarily on life as I fantasized it elsewhere, I chose to leave.

It does no good to think about what my life would have been like if I had not left home when I did, left the barrier island where so much had happened to my family's life, left the east coast.

I left for good. And the one who leaves is not the one who returns.

I moved away after graduating from high school and have not spent more than a week on the island ever since. My mother had wanted me to stay, attend Hofstra and live at home. She offered a new Ford Mustang, a monthly allowance, a paint job for my room, summer travel. She would ask no questions about my activities. She requested that my uncle talk to me about the future. She persuaded the family physician to counsel me. I remember the Rabbi was called.

To this day, I can't figure it. She'd always said she couldn't wait to have me out of the house for good. I had no respect for her things, was messy just like my brother and father had been, cared only for myself. I brought sand in from the beach. I liked to cook and she hated for me to cook, hated the mess that cooking made, hated my spills. We ate in restaurants or brought in prepared meals; we ate cold food, or—on rare occasions—things she could boil or sauté on the stove top. She stored Saltines and dry cereal in the unused oven, wrapped her pots and pans and china in plastic bags, covered unopened packages of cheese or lunch meat with layers of saran wrap. To get at the Raisin Bran, I had to take off an outer plastic bag, an inner plastic bag placed upside-down inside the first one, open the box, take out the plastic bag that held the cereal, untie the wire seal and have at it.

I felt that she'd be happiest if I could eat, sleep, shower and go to the bathroom somewhere else. Homework I could do on the premises. But no snacks and no music while I was at it.

I know many mothers say they can't wait for their teenaged children to be gone and may not really mean it. But my mother truly seemed to mean it; her words and actions had convinced me utterly. Besides, I'd heard her say the same things about my brother and I could tell she was very glad to have him out of the house.

When you're finally gone, she would say, I can have this place the way I always wanted it. I believed her.

But as my 18th birthday approached, she was changing her tune. She wanted me to stay?

I understand that she feared loneliness. With my father dead four years and my brother married three years, she would be on her own when I left. Also, as the youngest, my leaving would have signaled that a vital part of her life was over. But if she had not meant the things I heard her saying about me for so many years, things I accepted as fully as I accepted my name, then I didn't know what to believe.

✦

EVERY FEW years, I moved further west. In 1965, I went to Pennsylvania for college, living in the heart of Amish country. Four years later, I went to southern Illinois for graduate school, an area known as Little Egypt. We're talking about places vastly new and different from what I had known, places where my mother would never think of settling. I got married and later got my first real job in central Illinois, the Land of Lincoln, as a budget analyst on the Governor's staff. After seven years in Illinois, I relocated to Washington state—they called the gorgeous northwest landscape God's country—to work for the Appropriations Committee of the House of Representatives.

"You put a whole continent between us," my mother said in 1976. "I don't understand."

I thought I did.

Trained by profession to analyze complex problems, I thought I had this one all figured out. Getting as far away from home as possible, keeping a safe distance from a mother whose words and actions confused me, finding ever stranger landscapes to settle in, I was living life on my own terms. It never occurred to me that I might be hiding.

The movings continued. Oddly, for a while it seemed that I was tending toward home again. After two years in Washington, I moved back to central Illinois, which was proving to be the hub of my wanderings. At that rate, after a stint in Pennsylvania, I supposed I'd be settled in New York again by 1991.

But that didn't happen and it won't. In 1984, instead of moving to Pennsylvania again, I turned back to the west. I'm in Oregon to stay.

Now I wonder where I was going for a quarter century. I used to say "anywhere but home." I used to say "where the jobs were" and "where there are real seasons." When the elected leaders we worked for left office, my former wife and I looked for other elected leaders to work for. Packed up our kids and our possessions and headed out. Now I can see it never was an issue of going, but of following. I could not even imagine my own set of rules.

Sit, already, I finally told myself. Anywhere you want.

◆

FOR NEARLY two decades, the main piece of furniture in my various living rooms was a reupholstered hide-a-bed. We lived in a two-bedroom home at the time it was purchased—one bedroom for our son, the other for ourselves and our infant daughter. We bought the hide-a-bed when our daughter was old enough to sleep in a room of her own. We needed something to sleep on in the living room, not wanting our son to share his room with a baby who would wake him in the night.

There were also two butterfly chairs in the living room. We had their frames for years and made new covers for them when the old ones wore out. There were a couple of director's chairs too, which migrated to the porch each spring.

Furnishings from the American Cheesy School of interior decorating. My mother, when she saw a photograph taken in our living room, used the word *tacky*. The point is, my furnishings have not held much value for me.

This is no doubt a spillover from growing up in a kind of museum. I have tended to ignore the Things in my surroundings, to see a chair simply as something to sit in, the more worn the better. I am a notorious spiller of coffee and juice, a nicker of end tables and breaker of pottery. Our daughter's dog preferred the hide-a-bed's arms to his rawhide bones.

◆

I BROUGHT my daughter with me on the last visit home before I got sick. It was her spring break from high school, perhaps the last time Rebecca would be free and willing to travel with her father. She hadn't seen her grandmother in a half-dozen years.

This had become a sore point with me. Year after year, I offered to send her east for a visit. A week, a month, whatever my mother wanted. Let Rebecca have a dose of island life—the beach and boardwalk, clams on the half shell, salt air sticky on her ears. But my mother would never agree to it, was unwilling to have her there one-on-one. Kids were messy and demanding. So I decided to escort her there myself.

The three-room apartment where my mother had been living since she remarried is filled to bursting with bric-a-brac. Every piece I remember from my childhood seems to be there. The heavy brass footstool that no foot has ever rested on still gleams beside the old sofa, which has been recovered in an odd fabric of brown suede dappled with white leather. The little teak candy box that has never held candy and is too small for licorice twists, the abalone shell ashtrays that have never known ashes, the matchbox collection halted after my Bar Mitzvah in 1960, the piano and stool whose contents—sheet music of great Broadway melodies—remain wrapped in Saran Wrap. In the drawer of an end table she must have a hundred decks of lavishly illustrated playing cards, each stored in its own baggie. A wicker basket teems with eggs made of marble. The Henry Walton oil painting above her sofa has faded to the point where the figures are difficult to distinguish.

After hugging my mother, Rebecca walked to the middle of the living room and stood there, hands on hips, taking everything in. I saw her move toward the Roosevelt chair and knew she would plop into it without a second thought. I took my mother in my arms, glad to see her feeling well but also anxious to keep her turned away from what was about to happen in the room.

Later, sitting at the table in her tiny kitchen, we talked about how the town had changed. The young people had all gone away. The luxury resort hotels had become nursing homes, then way stations for the mentally ill, and now were being torn down for condominiums. The boardwalk is a patchwork of blond planks and salt rotted two-by-fours. The ski ball stalls sell shish-ka-bob in pita halves and the rusted gears of the ferris wheel weather near the beach like driftwood. An effort was underway to legalize gambling as a way of injecting revenue into the town. The most famous son is my high school friend Billy Crystal and every one of my classmates seems to have been at his Bar Mitzvah.

My thoughts returned to what my old teacher wrote about leaving. *Who is* the one who returns? At best, perhaps, he is the one who learns by having left. It took two decades, but I feel that I have grasped the notion of Home, the place that was the still point through all my wanderings and a focus of years of yearning thought. Home is, sadly enough, not the place I so much wanted my daughter to see, the place where my mother lived. It is the place I have made for myself in the world. Further, unless he's been run out of town, the one who returns is the one left free to choose, despite the pain his choices might cause. That has never been clearer to me than it has become since I got sick and my choices narrowed. I've also come to see that my mother could

have made it more difficult for me to leave than she did, finan-
cially as well as emotionally. And so the one who returns is, perhaps, the one who has come to accept—even himself—enough
to settle down.

✦

ALL MY life, I had fantasies of stripping the finish off the
Roosevelt chair. I would restore the original detail, loosen the
chair's tongue until the cane would sing under my weight.

It would take skills I didn't have, but that wouldn't stop me
from fantasizing. I could feel the bite of the sandpaper. Before
long, it would be me and Franklin again in the cold waters of the
Bay of Fundy.

I would sit in the chair and read while being warmed by the
first fire ever lit inside my mother's home. I would eat my dinner
in the chair: oozy food, purple food. I would drag it out to the
patio, change my children's diapers in it. Or I would keep it in
my writing room, sitting there like the President waiting for inspiration.

Me and my Roosevelt chair.

Now, in her mid-eighties, my mother calls to discuss nuances
of her will, to reveal the hidden locations of her treasures throughout the apartment, to be sure I want the things she wants me to
have. She promises that the chair will soon be mine.

And I tell her yes, I want it. I will keep it just the way it is.
Alas, however, I probably won't sit in it much because how would
my body feel after 140 straight days in the Roosevelt Chair?

6

Speaking of Grief

"I sometimes hold it half a sin
To put in words the grief I feel;
For words, like Nature, half reveal
And half conceal the Soul within."

—Alfred, Lord Tennyson
from "In Memoriam"

I FELT THE NEED to be by water. Having grown up on an island, having walked the beach during the eye of a hurricane and bobbed in the summery calm surf of an ocean at midnight, I felt something elemental tug at me when nothing else seemed able to reach through illness.

In August, 1990, I spent a week in a motel room on the Oregon coast. The closest town was named Rockaway. This was also the name of a narrow peninsula that lay just to the west of my child-hood home. But with its high-rise apartments, concrete handball courts and strip of filthy shoreline, the Rockaway of my youth didn't look anything like this one. Here there were stands of hem-lock and jack pine on the headlands, chunks of sandstone riddled by piddock clams, tidepools filled with starfish and sea anemones green as slices of kiwi fruit. I would allow myself a half hour to walk through foxglove and salal blossoms onto the beach, where I sat in a lair of driftwood watching the sun set across a nearly deserted stretch of strand. I'd have to be armed to try that back east.

The rear wall of the room was glass. I could see nearly to Tillamook Bay along a straight line of beach that, in the days before illness, I would have loved to run in the early morning light. I'd brought along a pair of binoculars and could scan the ocean to watch the fishing boats or check for migrating whales. Not very far out, two seastacks called Twin Rocks rose over a hundred feet at low tide. If they were twins, they sure weren't from the same egg. The one nearer shore was a jagged arch carved by years of wind and tide; a couple of boats could fit through its span, though not with much of a mast. Rising behind it, the second rock was a sleeping giant's head tilted back to catch the sun. Craggy, but stolid enough to sleep through centuries of storms. I liked to focus on the giant's head, trying to determine for sure if the little humps on its neck were a few small trees or seals. I really wanted them to be seals, despite the fact that they were in the same place all day for eight straight days.

This motel room in Rockaway was a perfect setting for the kind of thinking I felt compelled to do, which was about how I got to the place I found myself—in my early forties, disabled by a mysterious illness—and where to go from there. It was almost as if I could not begin to heal until I had grasped certain truths about myself, though I had no idea what those truths might be.

I did not believe I could make myself well, not by an act of will, not by clearer thinking. But I was beginning to believe that healing, on the one hand, and making myself well, *curing* myself, on the other hand, might be totally different things. Intuitively, I had known that I must start with first places, especially that narrow island in the Atlantic where I grew up.

Living in such a place implied the existence of faith. Every winter, the beach was flattened by breaking storm waves and eroded by surges and a fierce energy that filled the air with wind-blown sand, turning December's racket of surf into my child-hood's special white noise. After three or four months of that came hurricane season. A child there learned to believe. He learned to have faith in the return of summer swells sweeping sand up from the ocean floor. The longshore current that carried essential materials by which the beach rebuilt itself was an incar-nation of hope. There *would* be dunes again. There would be the soft, almost feminine profile of an August beach that I think I have always associated with the divine. Looking closely enough, a child on the island would witness a further miracle: the island literally rolled itself over in time, barrel staves from its bay side turning up embedded in the oceanfront. None of these things was visible as it happened, but nevertheless a person could see that it had indeed happened.

From the landscape of childhood, then, I believe I learned about endurance and constancy, about the steadfastness that un-derlies belief. I learned about the erosive power of implacable forces. But I also learned that things I could not see happened right before my eyes, so it was vital to study the world around me and grasp its essence if I wanted to avoid despair. I knew as if through my own body that healing comes from within, that there are always tests and to pass those tests you had to dig down, had to find resources in the very fabric of self.

On the island of my childhood, it was easy to equate the tem-pestuous, relentless presence of the sea with the Old Testament God I was learning about in the synagogue. God's harsh face and stormy presence. A God who was always testing and punishing, who destroyed whole cities with brimstone and fire or drowned the world in rain, who spoke to Job out of a whirlwind and Moses out of flame. This was the Lord of Personal Ordeals. King of Law and Commandment whose voice and visage were too much to bear. This was a God I think I felt in my bones. Such sto-ries, such images. Of course the God who turned father against son and brother against brother would later sacrifice a son of His own on a cross. This seemed consistent to someone who understood about power that followed its own ruthless dictates and distinguished nothing in its path. There was a picture in my synagogue of God materializing in long white flowing beard and robes, wrath crazing His brows, His lips pursed to suggest an imminent storm of rage. It was as though a child on the island could walk out of the turbulence of his religious studies directly into the very field of this same God's force. There might be trees blown flat by sea-laden winds, the skin of cars might be cankered by salt air, and everywhere there was the sound of pounding surf.

All this thinking about the island led me to remember again the last time I was actually there. It was that trip I took with my teenaged daughter about eight months before I got sick. Something vital happened there, something more important than letting my daughter sit in the Roosevelt chair, though I didn't recognize it at the time. I wish I had been more aware. Because I think there was a real opportunity to begin then the kind of healing that I am beginning now.

◆

MY DAUGHTER sang as she drove. This was our compromise. She'd wanted to listen to rock music; I'd wanted to listen to a Mets game. Rebecca's voice was lovely. It had been a long time since I heard her sing.

The Long Island highways, so familiar to me when I was her age, were alien to my daughter. But she didn't care. She was behind the wheel, the zany Long Island traffic didn't faze her, and our rental car was peppy.

We were taking the long way—the Meadowbrook to the Southern State—so that I could rattle off the names of towns and repeat anecdotes she hadn't heard in a good five years. We passed my high school, the field where I scored my first touchdown ("I know, Dad, it was a windy afternoon and you could hear the sand against your helmet"), the home of a girl I almost married, the toll booth where Sonny Corleone was ambushed in *The Godfather.*

"Exit here," I said, and she inclined her head my way. "Left at the light."

Pretty soon we were lost.

Of course I knew the name of the town where my father was buried! Of course I knew how to get there from my home town! But I was fourteen when he died and it had been a quarter century since I'd last been to the cemetery. Signs I expected to direct me were simply not around.

The signs that were around indicated Jamaicans and Haitians now called the town their home. We stopped at a gas station to ask directions.

"Which cemetery, Mon? Chewsh or de Catlick?"

✦

MY FATHER was a butcher. With his older brother, he'd inherited the family's wholesale poultry business when their father suddenly died.

The partnership didn't last long. According to my aunts, my father wanted the business to become modern. He reached out, got the Chinese restaurants to buy their chickens from him, sold all kinds of fowl, went retail. My uncle felt that what was good enough for Papa—the wholesale slaughter and distribution of poultry—was good enough for him.

The parting, however, was relatively amicable. My uncle and grandmother helped to finance the purchase of my father's market in the Battery section of Brooklyn. They were three equal-share partners in a corporation that owned the building and leased it to my father, who operated his live-poultry market there for nearly three decades. The arrangement worked well until my uncle and grandmother decided to raise my father's rent, forcing him to sell the business in 1957. It was then that we moved from

Brooklyn to Long Island and my father began his second career, at age 49, selling women's dresses in a business owned by his brother-in-law.

I have memories of spending occasional Saturday mornings at the chicken market with him. He would wake me in the dark, already dressed for work in clothes that would not show blood. When he flung open the market's gray metal doors, they rumbled in their tracks like train cars. The chickens would flap wildly when he approached, screaming "Help!" at the top of their lungs. The faces of three scales threw light back at me and became stars when I squinted. The floors were covered with fresh sawdust that would become patched with clots of feathers.

Through the streaked glass of his tiny office, I would watch him operate. He slipped a plaid flask of rye from beneath his apron to sip from in the cold morning air. He talked to the women who carried wire baskets like purses. He seized a plump pullet and dragged it feet first from the coop, tying it above the spurs, and dangled it from the scale. When the women nodded, he slit its throat and sent it back to the plucker, a one-armed man named Lefty. The bird came back, a spotted brown package, and the sale was rung.

My father was a busy man. He worked six days a week, leaving home in the dark and returning in the dark. He sat in his easy chair eating butterscotch cremes after supper, read the newspaper, sometimes went out to buy some cigars and surprise me with a few packs of baseball cards, then went to sleep. After a while, a time came when he wasn't allowed to eat candy any more. Sometimes, he would let me come into the bathroom with him so I could stick paper into a test tube of his urine and note what color it turned.

✦

ONE NIGHT my daughter modeled the gown my mother had worn on her wedding night. Rebecca came dancing into the living room, trailed from the bedroom by her beaming grand-mother. The handmade lace had aged, but its silk fit Rebecca like a second skin. This, I learned, is what comes from having a seam-stress sew on the bias.

I did not know which one to watch—the young woman twirling through a shaft of moonlight, or the doyenne in a house-coat who clung fifty years to her finery hoping for this very night. Rebecca seemed a torso taller than my mother and half her weight. I did not see how everything could fit.

Off they went and back they came. This time Rebecca was in the dress my mother wore for my brother's Bar Mitzvah. Next time she wore a cotton sari with one end draped over her head. Soon there were jewels, gloves, a voluminous plastic parka.

Finally, I followed them back to the secret chamber. Between them, my mother's dresser teemed with apparel. Scarves unfurled stories she'd waited years to tell. Blouses revealed secrets I'd never heard before. In one corner of the closet, I saw the ermine coat and stole my grandfather made for her when my mother was Rebecca's age, his verve and artistry woven through its perfect seams.

I knew we would be taking more things home than we had room for in our bags. I also knew Rebecca wouldn't wear them back in Oregon. But there was nothing to say. It was clear that this stuff needed to head west. I walked over to the bed and picked up a leather jacket brought home from Rome the month before my father's death.

My mother coddled a burnt umber heap until it became the jumper she'd worn in *South Pacific*. She sang while she smoothed out its matching shawl, draping it over Rebecca's shoulders. It was a song I remembered my mother singing to me at bedtime. I had sung it to Rebecca hundreds of times. We stood there hold-ing vintage clothing in our hands, singing together of enchanted evenings.

◆

MY DAUGHTER's song faded as she steered through the gates. She stopped where the main office squatted like a shrine. A driveway forking into narrow tines made it clear yet again that I could not direct her to my father's grave.

It was the end of winter. Browned grass contrasted with ground cover green and thick as memory. We opened the car doors into silence.

Inside the office, a man in dreadlocks called my father's name up on his screen. He smiled at my daughter, then marked our map with an orange line that led to the cemetery's edge. She drove slowly on a road too narrow for turning back. This was it. I recognized the place in bright rushes, although it was smaller and more crowded than I remembered. But its shapes were more austere.

When Uncle George died, I lived a continent away and didn't come home for the funeral. The Washington Legislature was in session; I was on the staff and couldn't take the time off. When Uncle Saul died, aboard a ship en route to Naples, no one could say for sure when he'd actually get home for burial. He landed as cargo and had to be shipped to Genoa first, so it would be tricky to make airline reservations. The west coast cousins chipped in and bought one ticket to New York—cousin Richard was our designated mourner.

Since my father's death I had come here only twice. The first time was for the unveiling of his headstone and the other, three years later, was for the burial of my grandmother. Now I could taste the familiar hush. I could touch the scent of forgotten mornings when, as a little boy, I'd been here with my father to visit his father's grave. There was a sound of whispered prayer again in the wind.

My daughter stepped into the family plot for the first time, older than I was when my father died. For reasons I did not yet understand, the cemetery was something I'd always kept to myself. No one in the life I had made without him had been here with me.

◆

A QUARTER century smoothes even the most jagged images. I remembered the rectangle of earth breached in rain, the hole a glazed well, and a fistful of dirt pitched after him.

I also remembered that every evening for a year after he died, I had attended services to pray for my father. It was a job handed to me by my older brother and my uncles. I didn't understand why so much praying was necessary, but I did believe that failure to do it would have terrible consequences for my father's eternal rest.

Month after month, I rode my bicycle to the synagogue just before sundown to join the old men in mourning. I was the only teenager among them. Indeed, there was only one other man younger than seventy who attended regularly during the year. We were a community of grievers; it was required that ten of us be present for the prayers to be said.

I failed my father twice. The first time was in a blizzard, when the old men could not come out of their homes. We did not make our ten man quorum. I'd ridden to the synagogue and waited with the Rabbi in his office, crying as I watched the sun set. He assured me it would be all right to pray alone that night, but I was never convinced.

The second time was late spring. I was on the school baseball team and we had an out-of-town game that went into extra innings. On the bus ride home, realizing I wouldn't make it to the synagogue by sundown, I could not control my tears. The coach sat next to me the whole way back, explaining that winning should not be that important to me.

◆

MY FATHER's headstone leaned toward a space between him and his brother. It was space that was waiting to be filled with my mother. There was a marble slab seat etched with our name that sat obliquely on its base. I centered it and settled down beside my daughter.

"Look!" she whispered, pointing to her great-grandfather's headstone. "He was born on my birthday."

I hadn't known that.

Her great-grandmother, Katie Tatarsky from Bialystok, Poland, and her dour look came back clearly when I considered her marble stone. She would be 102. That fact astonished me. I hadn't thought about her in years. She'd married my grandfather when she was 17, after he'd left the underwear factory and opened a grocery store. It was her expertise that got them into the poultry business. My daughter had never known her.

There was a red disc fixed to the family marker looming above the headstones. The disc hovered at the marker's edge like a disappearing sun. Across the center like clouds were the letters "PC."

"Maybe it means they've got the plot on their computer," my daughter said.

"I think it means the family bought Perpetual Care." I waved my hand toward the adjacent plot, which looked overgrown and abandoned. "That explains why our bushes and vines are so trim."

For a while, we sat with our arms entwined and said nothing. Our breath was visible in the air. We agreed it was strange that our people all seemed to be born in the autumn. We agreed that winter was the worst season for them. We said it was good to be here.

Then she stood. She took a camera from her purse, and walked backwards to get perspective on the scene.

While my daughter took snapshots, I thought about what we had said. It *was* good to be here together, but I couldn't yet say why.

✦

THE NATURALIST John Muir observed, in *A Thousand-Mile Walk to the Gulf,* that "On no subject are our ideas more warped and pitiable than on death." He goes on to urge us to let children "see the beautiful blendings and communions of death and life, their joyous inseparable unity, as taught in woods and meadows, plains and mountains and streams of our blessed star, and they will learn that death is stingless indeed, and as beautiful as life, and that the grave has no victory, for it never fights. All is divine harmony."

Do people really come to believe that? Beautiful blendings, stingless death, divine harmony? At age forty, sitting there in the chilly morning air between my father's grave and my daughter's blossoming figure, I felt utterly confused.

I wondered what I knew, after all. It is important to accept the fact of death, the certainty that fathers are mortal. It is important to honor our dead, to remember them. I'd written about these matters for years, only I hadn't done anything about them. Hadn't acted; just knew, just wrote.

About sex, about surviving on long hikes, about how to drive a car, I'd done a much better job. I'd been open and patient with my children, explained, answered questions, encouraged. We practiced going to hospitals for weeks before my son had his tonsils out. Each time we moved across the country, we did things right—flew together to the new city for inspection, packed together, practiced smaller relocations by camping our way to the new home.

But visit my father's grave? Why lug the children there as my father lugged me? It wasn't such a big deal. Besides the vivid sense of the place, its sights and smells, what I remembered most clearly from visiting here when my father was alive was wondering whether I could jump over my grandfather's headstone. The whole practice seemed pointless and a bit morbid.

✦

REBECCA CAME back to me. I sensed that she didn't know whether it was all right to smile, to hug me then, to say something soothing. Looking at her, my confusion began to lift. I realized what had been wrong and what had been missing. In keeping this experience from her for so long, in hoarding the sadness, I had in truth been refusing to share something vital of myself with her.

When my father died, pulled from the swimming pool where he'd had his heart attack and drowned, I'd been too stunned at first to grieve. Then I found a ready format, a procedure. My duty was assigned to me and I did it. Next, having followed the rules, I turned away from grief and got on with my life.

What I talked about, when I talked about my father's death at all, was that I feared dying young myself. I didn't talk much about his life because I didn't know much about his life. I didn't talk about how I felt when he died because I didn't know how I felt when he died.

It must have seemed that his death had only happened to him, when, in fact, his death had happened to me too. Maybe silence made it seem that my father meant so little to me that his loss wasn't devastating.

Now I stood and took my daughter in my arms. In the vault of my heart, I'd always known where the sudden deaths of fathers left the lives of their children. Maybe I wanted to spare her a glimpse of that knowledge. But the real truth was that, in lieu of my father's sustaining love, I had been clinging to grief. No one was fooled except me. Rather than suggesting that my father's loss was no big deal, my actions suggested that all we ultimately have from our fathers is their loss. Perhaps a few mementos, a few memories, stories that we can tell—but primarily loss. This must have seemed why my most lasting emotion was a grief I would not share, and therefore maybe did not really feel. I realized that I want the children to have more of me.

In the end, even the truest of stories can turn like a skewed shadow. This could either be from the angle of light or the angle of view. Or perhaps something within the story itself causes it suddenly to turn, to change course against the light. Skewed shadows are difficult to catch right.

But after that trip home, at least I knew what I knew, even if I didn't know how to do anything about it. As they often do, however, things quickly returned to normal.

Within eight months, I was sick. It was difficult to explain to my children what was wrong with me, difficult to hold them close enough to the experience of being ill for so long while they charged through their teenage years. I was just there, changed utterly, a somber presence.

Two years later, I was a participant in the Ampligen study, volunteering my body for the trial of a drug that might help me. Part of the screening process involved undergoing a lumbar puncture. Commonly known as a spinal tap, this procedure mimics the way sap is extracted from a sugar maple tree—and feels about as crude. I curled into the fetal position so that a long, fine bore needle could be inserted between two vertebrae and passed into the spinal canal, where a small amount of the fluid which bathes my brain and spinal cord was removed. This procedure would permit measurement of my intracranial pressure, which was very high, and analysis of my cerebrospinal fluid, which showed twice the normal level of protein. Beforehand, I did everything I had been instructed to do—hydrating as though before a marathon, using my best relaxation techniques, visualizing an easy time of it. Although the tap itself was not exceptionally painful, the aftermath was a disaster.

I followed my doctor's post-tap instructions as faithfully as I'd followed his preparatory instructions. I remained in bed, drank gargantuan amounts of liquid, rested. It was terribly hot that week, upper nineties, but my bedroom was comfortably air-conditioned. However, three days after the procedure, I was brought by a friend to the hospital's emergency room incoherent and continually repeating the sentence "How could it be August 8?" Dehydrated, with an agonizing headache, a leaky tap-site and probably some kind of reaction to pain medication, I was having what my doctor called "a neurological event." I spent four hours on a gurney in the corner of the emergency room receiving intravenous solutions and sleeping.

From their homes on opposite sides of Portland, my children rushed up to Oregon Health Sciences University after being notified by their mother. My first memory of that entire day is waking up to see my son walking out of the room and my daughter walking in. Noticing that I was awake, she grabbed his arm as they passed one another and spun him around.

"Hey!" all three of us said at once.

They stayed with me for a few minutes, despite the hospital's rule about one visitor in ER at a time. They explained what had happened, what the doctor had explained to them, asked how I felt, studied the various tubes stuck into me, touched my face, told me not to move yet. I was too dried out to cry, but felt overwhelmed with gratitude at being alive and seeing their faces. I told them so.

My illness had been difficult for them. I realized that I had been so wrapped up in how difficult it was for me and in trying to shield them from worry, I had not made them understand what was happening. There were, instead, brief reports of facts, of tests and results, status updates. Life went on. Besides, I did not look particularly sick. I had an illness few people understood, but which simply sounded as though I was tired. Big deal. Suddenly I could no longer run with my son, as I had done for so many years, even after he married. My daughter would come home from school with her friends and there I was all the time, in my recliner, impinging on her freedom, needing quiet. It was not long before she had moved into an apartment of her own, and I was feeling more and more cut off from both of them. A situation such as this compounds the normal stress of separating from grown children while at the same time adding to the confusion of sudden and mysterious illness, a nasty cycle.

Yet here we were, the three of us gathered together in mutual concern, support, and love. This was something my father's early, sudden death had denied him and me. It was precious, a kind of blessing out of the chaos of my illness, a reprise of the lessons from that earlier trip to the cemetery, and I was not about to let it go without saying something clear this time.

"I'm so grateful you both came," I said for starters.

"Be quiet," my daughter said.

"See if you can pee in this bottle yet," my son said.

PART THREE

While the Exorcist Drowses

"Someone has suddenly fallen ill and one summons the exorcist. Since he is not at home, one has to send messengers to look for him. After one has had a long fretful wait, the exorcist finally arrives, and with a sigh of relief one asks him to start his incantations. But perhaps he has been exorcizing too many evil spirits recently; for hardly has he installed himself and begun praying when his voice becomes drowsy."

—Sei Shōnagon (tenth-century Japan)
from *The Pillow Book*, "Hateful Things"

7

Honeymooning with the Feminine Divine

I FLEW INTO tomorrow to see the face of the Divine. Nothing else had worked.

Door to door, the trip lasted twenty-five hours and I arrived awfully tired to be taking in such a sight. She sat in a white leather armchair surrounded by roses and tulips, nodding as in a trance, and looked back at me with enormous brown eyes. Then I went back to my folding chair and sat down. I did not throw away my cane and skip from the room healed, though I wouldn't have objected. There had been no great conflagration of light, nor had my past slipped away from me like a dream. My wife Beverly put her hand over mine and squeezed. What seemed divine right then was the thought of a bed and feather pillow.

So I had traveled all that way and felt nothing. Maybe it was jet lag. Maybe I needed to work into it gradually. At least we would be around for seven more of these encounters before it was time to leave Germany.

Of course I hadn't expected to be alone with this woman many call The Divine Mother. Beverly was there too (this was our honeymoon) and so was her best friend Ishara (this was our honeymoon?). But neither had I expected to be sharing the experience with a hundred seventy other people. Maybe that was why I didn't feel anything during this first visit. Too much going on, too much energy in the space. I looked around the room, which must have been the house's original combined living and dining rooms. Old hippies and a teenager in pink dreadlocks, a child of nine, a couple nearing eighty. There were men in suits, men in cut-off sweat shorts, men dressed as for the opera. There were women in overalls or floor-length skirts, women who looked as though they'd spent all day trading securities. A stocky, bearded man with two prosthetic legs had to reach down and lock himself upright after kneeling before her. Out in the parking lot beforehand, I had heard German, French, Italian and Dutch. There were British, Israelis, Africans and Indians. Inside, in this room with its white marble tiles on the floor, white flocked wallpaper and a ceiling panelled in wood stained white, a lot of people wept. No one had trouble being silent for the three hours it took to get one minute of her gaze and touch.

◆

THE DAY we had left Oregon for Germany, I had been sick for almost five years and married for five days. A disabled Brooklyn-born Jew living with my bride in her round house in the woods, I went to a tiny village in the Westerwald during a spring of violent German anti-foreigner activity in order to see an Indian avatar while on my honeymoon with the maid-of-honor along as chaperon.

If nothing else, this would seem to prove I am either a man of some faith, at my wit's end, or nuts. I prefer to say it proved I was willing to take risks and was open to wonder. I know I was ready for anything.

Months before, I had read that the feminine divine—the Divine Mother—is more loving and soft, more patient and more accepting than the typical masculine divine. Understand this was not my typical sort of reading material. I prefer to mix contemporary poetry and novels with a bi-monthly dose of classic fiction, a quarterly biography, the occasional dollop of thriller or mystery, and magazines for relish. But Beverly had these books about the feminine divine lying around and as we'd grown closer I thought it would be good to see what had moved her so deeply.

Her books said that the Divine Mother appears on earth to give help for physical, mental, vital and spiritual well-being, to give peace and to help people obtain their needs. Sounded just right to me, though far outside my familiar frame of reference. Arthur Schopenhauer, one of my early favorites on this topic, said in *On Religion*, "The fundamental distinction between religions does not lie in whether they are monotheistic, polytheistic, pantheistic or atheistic, but in whether they are optimistic or pessimistic." The God of my childhood, God the Father, was strict and vengeful, a God of laws and penalties, and although Schopenhauer also said "the basic character of Judaism is *realism* and *optimism*," I had not found it so. I had not been in my God's house since 1962, but I knew it was time for help. Time for some optimism.

In Beverly's books, I had read that there are several incarnations of the Divine Mother among us now. Avatars, they work to heal or protect or transform. This one—the one Beverly had been reading about for a year or so—is known to her followers as Mother Meera, which means both *wonder* and *miracle*. The books said she lives at Oberdorf 4a in the little German village of Dornburg-Thalheim, and quoted Mother Meera as saying, "The Divine is the sea. All religions are rivers leading to the sea. Some rivers wind a great deal. Why not go to the sea directly?"

Ok, I thought, I will. In my place, you might have done the same thing.

Of course, there were lots of questions. Could I physically make such a trip and be in any condition to face her? Would she make me well? Would she bless my marriage and my work? Perhaps most vital of all, would I hide behind a wall of skepticism, would I believe my eyes or believe my heart?

✦

FOR NEARLY five years, there had been so much wrong with my physical being that I didn't pay attention to my spiritual being. This is odd, I know. Many people in my situation would look to their spirituality for direction or support. My illness wasn't likely to kill me; it had utterly changed my life, taken me out of my life, but it wasn't thought to be terminal.

My response was to study up on viruses and immune cells, to read about pharmaceuticals, herbs and enzymes. The crisis, I felt, was medical. I visualized. I volunteered for experimental therapies, took every drug that had ever been tried with my illness and a couple that had not. I took vitamins and minerals. There was a course of acupuncture; there were massage, naturopathics, homeopathics. I did a fourteen-week stint in a pilot program at the Oregon Health Sciences University that combined occupational therapy with nutrition advice, group interaction, and counseling on the subject of managing chronic illness.

Somehow, during the first five years of illness I just never got around to issues of the spirit. To me, my health was not a matter of faith or holiness, it was a matter of pathogens and Memory T Cells and Interleukin Receptors. It was a matter of treatment, of cure. And if I had gotten around to issues of the spirit, I doubt I'd have imagined going to Germany to visit an avatar as a way of addressing those issues.

◆

WE TRAVELED light, one backpack each. I wore pants so festooned with pockets that I could carry on my person a thick packet of airline tickets, various currencies separated by country, traveler's checks with their receipts dutifully stored in a different place, passport, a German dictionary to refresh my memory on vocabulary, brochures and confirmations concerning our lodging, a fat novel to read, two sandwiches and, if I'd wanted to, an entire orchard of fruits. The pants drooped almost off my hips, despite the belt that cinched them tight enough to leave a scar.

Friday, an illusion, simply vanished as we headed for Frankfurt, nine time zones east of home. We talked a lot about home, that small round structure Beverly had built four years ago in the middle of twenty hilly, wooded acres. It had been joyful for us to be married there, in a space without edges, our families in attendance. We followed a ceremony concocted together with the husband and wife chaplain team that married us, the view of oak and fir nearly obscured by the six-foot eight-inch Bert fumbling through his notes. *Now Ishara will read a poem by Rainier Wilkie.*

Over the mid-Atlantic, there were three hours of fitful sleep, which I counted as the first miracle of our trip since we were surrounded by a jetful of babies screaming in carefully coordinated sequence. I had been certain there would be no sleep at all. Amity to Portland to Seattle to Copenhagen to Frankfurt. Then we rented a car and drove an hour north on the Autobahn to our Pension in tiny Elbtal. Miracle Number Two was that Beverly could drive our tiny Opal on the Autobahn after such a long day of flying, with me in the backseat translating road signs and folding and refolding the Euro Cart map, which was roughly the size of our down comforter. Not only do drivers go insanely fast on the Autobahn, they like to get close enough to inspect your luggage while zooming up behind you.

Miracle Number Three was the Pension Russman itself. It was

a converted mill—the *Untere Gadelheimer Muhle* or Lower Gadelheimer Mill to be exact—and was so verdantly picturesque that we had to laugh when we first drove up. Why, we couldn't even find the Upper Gadelheimer Mill from there because the Pension was nestled in a wooded field beside a stream and all we could see out back was Nature in shameless display. Like Ishara's room directly below, our's overlooked a verdant stretch of back acreage lush with trees and cut by waters babbling over strategically placed rocks. Birds, every herb known to man, irises, rhododendron, pond plants in bloom, even a gentle breeze through the open windows. It bordered on too much.

We'd been greeted at the door by Ursula Russman, effusive and warm, eager to be of help, as full of life as the land she lived on. Even if I hadn't been exhausted, my college German was about as effective as Frau Russmann's English. But we seemed able to understand one another well enough. Though Herr Russmann spoke excellent English, he worked in Frankfurt all day and would not be around to translate. When he was, I rendered him speechless with laughter by confusing a Geflugelhof (poultry farm) with a Flugelhof (airport). Hell, they both have to do with wings.

We unpacked quickly and lay down for a nap prior to our first visit to Mother Meera, but the damn cuckoo clocks throughout the Pension were broken. They went off constantly, and unless it was truly twenty-nine o'clock, they had lost all track of time. When we finally went downstairs to leave just before six, we asked Frau Russmann about her clocks and learned that what we'd been hearing was in fact real birds. Cuckoos actually existed. That was only the beginning.

◆

MOTHER MEERA does her work in silence. "People are too active and rarely sit quietly," she has said. "In silence one can receive more because all one's activities become concentrated." She offers no lectures or discussion groups; there is no proselytizing, no outreach. Instead, four evenings a week people can sit in her house without talking from seven till about ten as, one by one, each gets a chance to be before her. It lasts a little longer than an opera, with no music and nothing happening on stage.

Even without Chronic Fatigue Syndrome, it would not be easy to sit that long on a small folding chair "with nothing to do." I myself am a spot-reader; I like to carry a book to read anywhere, at any time, if I anticipate even a brief period "with nothing to do." Waiting for my haircut, coming attractions to begin in the movie theater, the bus to arrive, water to boil. Sometimes I will take a book into the bathroom when I floss and brush my teeth, so I can have "something to do." The prospect of sitting for three hours—unable to talk to Beverly, unable to read or write in my notebook, no bathroom break or intermission—was daunting. Since getting sick, I had learned to meditate and had gotten to perhaps the Advanced Beginner stage, definitely not adept enough for three hours worth.

On the second evening at Oberdorf 4a, I was better organized. I had sat through that one session already, loopy with fatigue, astounded by the crowd, and at least now I understood the rhythm of the process. If I was mystified by what Beverly and Ishara said they had experienced the night before, by their ecstasy and clarity of insight, by what they had felt and seen, at least I had some idea of what to expect in the room.

We settled into our seats and I looked around, trying hard not to stare. Most people already had their eyes closed, hands palm-up on their knees, thumb and forefinger forming a circle. They were nodding to themselves, serenely smiling. A few people sat on the floor on small pillows, legs folded lotus-style. Beside me, Beverly was transported, turned wholly inward it seemed, and so beautifully at rest that it took my breath away. Beside her, eyes flickering as though in sleep, Ishara was beaming. I was rested enough from yesterday's travels and initial exposure to be concerned: what if nothing happens, what if I cannot sit through another three-hour session, what if I lose my balance when I approach her and land in her lap? Could happen, and probably will if I close my eyes.

At precisely seven, Mother Meera came down from her upstairs living quarters and entered the packed, hushed room. Looking neither trifling nor delicate, she was nevertheless slight. Take it from a man who since Kindergarten has stood at the front of every line organized by size, the woman was small, but her self-containment and aura of resolution produced a large presence. If she were to be drawn in caricature, she would be composed primarily of eyes and lips, the rest of her face dark and indistinct, and her womanly body would be shrouded in a bright sari—purple or burgundy or blue, each tinged with gold. Everybody stood as she moved to her armchair. Everybody sat when she sat.

There were no lines or numbers as at a deli counter, no set order or procedure for getting to come before her, yet people seemed to cooperate without communicating. They flowed steadily toward and away from her, replacing one another in the straight-backed chair to her left that served as a kind of holding tank, then a minute later coming before her as the previous person returned to his or her original place in the room. A ballet, say *The Dance of Blessing*, achieved in silence except for the shuffling of feet, the click of joints or creak of chair, an occasional sob or sharp intake of breath.

I could feel a change in the room's very air as the first hour waned. Tension and excitement, at first fairly palpable despite everyone's efforts at meditative calm, began to ebb. People grew intensely serene, if such a thing is possible, and the air was still throughout the second hour, like a coastal evening in the time between two weather fronts. The crowd seemed to glow, to be deeply eased, individuals settling into themselves both physically and psychically, elated but tranquil. I stole glances and wondered what was going on for them. The warm summer air began to cool at just the right time for the crowded room and a breeze moved through the open windows as though on order. In the third hour, however, the toll of prolonged sitting began to tell, eroding slightly the peace and stillness. People struggled to respect the needs of those who had yet to approach her, but there was more movement to be felt, more physical energy, more coughs.

As the evening progressed, I could not decide when to stand and move toward Mother Meera. This of course seemed an indication that I was not quite with the program yet. I ought to know intuitively, as everyone else seemed to know, precisely when it was my moment to approach her. Earlier, over dinner at the Italian restaurant in Elbtal where everyone spoke only German, Ishara had talked about what she was going to ask for when she was with Mother Meera. *If you want anything—love, truth, or courage, for example—you must ask for it.* It was not that Ishara saw Mother Meera as a kind of Santa Claus, but rather that she perceived the nature of the feminine divine's giving as fundamentally nurturant and beneficent. Mother Meera was there to assist—*I am looking at everything within you to see where I can help, where I can give healing and power*—so perhaps it made sense to let her know what you needed. Beverly's approach was to work on the intention to surrender, to become an empty vessel and remain open. *It depends on your sincerity, aspiration and love.* I wondered how to express to Mother Meera what I needed, how to formulate the mixture of desires, preferably in priority order since she seemed to have a lot on her hands these days, without hogging up all the air between us.

But I was having trouble because the whole notion suddenly seemed base to me. Trundle off to Germany, ask the Divine Mother to help you get well and maybe sell your novel while she's at it. I had thought about it earlier and believed I came to her in good faith, willing to be open and to surrender myself to what was going on. But now that I was in her presence there was a strong feeling of doubt. I wanted to be honest and honorable. Suppose I came before her filled with uncertainty about what I was doing there and she looked within me to see . . . what? Uh, Mother Meera, it's about my health, then there's this wonderful love with Beverly that I'd like you to bless or whatever, and I've got a book that just came out which I'd appreciate your making sure a lot of people get to read, and could you also help me get clear about this matter of the spiritual life.

I got up just after the man with prosthetic legs and before the woman in a wheelchair. Without thinking about it in these terms, I must have felt kinship, as though we were the Crip Brigade. I watched the man carefully to see what he did. After he rose, he reached down to lock his knees in place and backed away. Then I stood, holding onto the cane till my balance was steady and I felt safe moving in front of her armchair. I knelt, laying the cane across my knees, and bent my head between Mother Meera's knees. She gripped the sides of my head. The impulse was to shut my eyes, but I knew that if I did I would topple forward into her lap.

What popped into mind, as I knelt there looking at the white leather an inch from my nose and thinking about health, love, novels and spirit, surprised the hell out of me. *Help me to see how it all fits together.*

She released my head. I rocked back onto my haunches and looked into her eyes, too stunned even to wonder about whether it was okay to blink.

✦

THE NEXT night, Sunday, we were shifted out of sight. Because we had already attended two sessions and newcomers deserved spots where they could see Mother Meera, we had to sit in a back room. Jammed together on the floor of a small parlor, backs against walls with nothing but the opposite wall to look at, we had no view of Mother Meera and could feel no breeze. My body was not cooperating. Three hours were going to last six. I tried to recall the wedding procession we had seen that afternoon in Thalheim, the radiant bride leading a march through the village, the number of her escorts swelling as she turned this way and that. It seemed as though we met up with her everywhere while we strolled in search of a place to eat, no matter which streets we followed, no matter how far in the opposite direction we seemed to be going. But the images did not do much to speed the passage of time. Meanwhile, Beverly and Ishara seemed able to pick up what they called Meera Energy from the very air and, though they were uncomfortable, were getting as much from the experience as they had the previous nights. Eyes closed, concentrating, they were moved and at peace. I squirmed like a five-year-old boy, though I tried not to. Bones and joints aflame, muscles twitching like Christmas tree lights along the outline of my skeleton, I found myself transported all right—transported back to our home in the woods, wondering what had come in the mail that day.

Suddenly a hand touched my shoulder. It belonged to one of Mother Meera's associates, a sweet-tempered young German named Michael who met the visitors each night in the parking lot to divide them into groups and dispatch them to Oberdorf 4a. A place had been found for me in the main room. For the remainder of our visits, I would be permitted to come directly to the house without having to stand in the parking lot beforehand and to sit wherever I was comfortable. To me, this seemed an exquisite kindness and I was grateful. To Beverly, who had spent her time in the room invoking Mother Meera's help on my behalf, it seemed like the arrival of grace, an immediate answer to her prayers.

Sunday night, the dreaming began. Most of my life, I've been subject to night terrors and would waken whoever shared my bed with moans that apparently sound like a ghost is loose in the room, though to me it is definitely the repeated word HELP!

Doctors say night terrors come from a different sleep stage than dreams. They are hallucinations, not nightmares; the state of fear and agitation they leave the dreamer in is intense because the distorted images are so vivid, absolutely real. Mine always take the form of a relentless chase. I slow down till I'm reduced to clawing along the street on hands and knees trying to escape. Sometimes they might be set on city streets, others in the desert or on a mountain side. No matter where they are set, there are always the stalkers, anonymous and grim. If there was no one else in bed I would awaken myself, the sounds finally audible even to me, and lie there with a pounding heart, bathed in sweat. According to the literature, night terrors are more common in children. But I had had them periodically all my life until getting sick, when sleep disturbance, a hallmark of Chronic Fatigue Syndrome, caused all my dreaming to cease. The stalker had caught me.

The dreams in Germany were slightly different, as I tried to explain to Beverly in the middle of the night after she had awakened me to stop the noises and gasps. She moved her long body very close, covering every inch of mine with her warmth. Since our faces were close together, her feet stretched about five inches past mine and I had the sense that the whole bed was suffused with my wife's loving presence. The dreams were specific, set in the apartment I remembered from my childhood in Brooklyn. They culminated in my being trapped behind an open door while the stalkers moved in on me. And the stalkers were not anonymous. They were quite clearly my parents.

Within twenty minutes, Beverly had the whole thing explained to me. Why did the dreams resume now? Because Mother Meera had seen and understood. I was being shown the way. Perhaps I should put aside the novel I had begun, about a man who becomes a human medical research subject, and instead write the novel I needed to write. The one I'd stopped five years ago after three chapters because I could not handle the material. A novel about my childhood, about abuse.

◆

MONDAY I felt ill, unable to leave the Pension even for my daily walk through the woods and fields between Elbtal and Ellar. We had anticipated such days would come during the trip and had a plan for them, but I was saddened to be in Germany and be confined to bed. I read John Gardner, with whom I had studied nearly a quarter century before, and listened to cuckoos. In the evening, Beverly and Ishara went to see Mother Meera without me, while I sat outside the garage with the Russmanns for a warm three-hour visit. They provided me with the entire history of the mill and their tenure as owners. In a wondrous mix of languages, we addressed most of the issues concerning the influx of foreigners and Germany's staggering economy, nodding vigorously at each other's insights.

From Tuesday till Friday, when the next set of four evenings with Mother Meera would begin, Beverly and I had a solo honeymoon trip to the Rhine and Moselle. We saw the Lorelei at Saint Goarshausen and gazed at the romantic river, which was actually frantic with industrial traffic. Then it was so hot in Zell that school had been canceled, I got my beard perfectly trimmed by a smiling old man whose hands trembled while he worked, and I believe that I should not tell you any more about our little interlude than that.

Attending three of the final four visits with Mother Meera, I had time to sit in Oberdorf 4a for a few minutes before the others arrived. I chose a different seat each night, hoping to get an alternative perspective on what occurred in the room. I thought about asking for clarification about my dreams, or repeating the spontaneous request for help in seeing how the pieces of my hopes fit together. I thought about making myself an empty, open vessel. But I must say that nothing significant happened, unless improvement at managing to sit for three hours constitutes something significant.

Which is, of course, exactly the point. The divine, the essence of spirituality, comes out of living everyday life closely. It is not necessary that much happen, except the finding of greater awareness. I think ideas like "the divine" or "spirit" were in many ways fearsome ideas for me. I had done without God for more than half my life. My reading and education had somehow led me to believe that such ideas lined a path of intellectual weakness. Like New Age music, which I always referred to as "woo-woo music," and self-help books, they indicated a softness at the center.

Now I am not proclaiming any major spiritual breakthrough from my visit to Mother Meera. Day to day, my outward life has not changed appreciably, though there are times I find myself thinking about Mother Meera's eyes and the touch of her hands on my head, even asking her for help now and then. I did not come home to set up an altar in the living room or begin reading the Tibetan Rinpoches. But I did come home and within three months had completed a novel about child abuse called *The Open Door*. Shortly after that, I realized that the dreams had been so transformed as to be essentially gone. On rare nights, the ghosts still do appear in our bedroom, but the chase is over and there are no stalkers. One night, I turned on them; in the dream, the word I was yelling when Beverly woke me was GO! Another night, my twenty-one year old daughter was trapped in an elevator and I was trying to get her. The words were HOLD ON!

Like Beverly and Ishara, I had first read about Mother Meera as most people do, through *Hidden Journey* by British poet and novelist Andrew Harvey. His book vividly describes his encounters with Mother Meera beginning in 1978 and his spiritual development in her presence. Harvey makes an observation that is coming to feel appropriate for me as well: "All my life I had worked with words, wanted to use them, to master them; nearly everything I had learned had come to me through words. But in Meera's silence I returned to a deeper learning, the one I experienced in music when my whole being was addressed."

8

Home Remedies

"Diseases desperate grown
By desperate appliance are relieved,
Or not at all."

—William Shakespeare, from *Hamlet*

THE FIRST CALL was about garlic. The man said he knew how to cure me. He said that all I had to do was follow his instructions for one month. Thirty days, Fred, he said. *What have you got to lose?*

Because I had published essays and appeared on television talk-shows devoted to the subject of my illness, in 1990 I was becoming a famous sick person. The poet Byron has said "fame is the thirst of youth," but this was not the way my youthful cravings for fame had looked—till my early twenties I had dreams of playing left field for the Dodgers or starring in a string of funny but poignant films. No, I had known for a long time that, as Byron also said, fame was like "climbing up a hill, whose summit, like all hills, is lost in vapor." It was enough for me to be appreciated by whatever readers my poems and novels would find. The dream now was that Billy Crystal will read one of those novels and decide to make a movie out of it, expanding both my readership and my wallet. However, three years have passed since I sent him the first one and I am still waiting to hear how he likes it.

My decision to go public with my illness was a very conscious one, but it was not driven by the desire for fame. When I first got sick, my illness was so poorly understood by the public and media, which thought of it as The Yuppie Flu, and so mishandled by the medical community, which had trouble diagnosing and believing in it, that I felt the need to let them all know what was really involved. I was driven by the desperate desire to communicate.

Now the communication loop was coming back toward me. So as the man on the phone said, what did I have to lose? He told me to peel a garlic clove by clove and swallow each clove whole until I had to stop. Then I should dice the rest into tablets I could gulp down with the help of raw milk. Since a person in my circumstances can never get too much garlic, I should also rub split cloves into the creases of my skin, grind some to a powder I breathe deeply in, take long garlic baths, burn garlic incense and drink dark garlic tea. I should wear long garlic amulets everywhere. Most of all, what he would really recommend is that I let him come to my house and show me the proper way to use garlic cloves dipped in oil as suppositories.

Within weeks, I was overwhelmed with remedies. A woman who had been ill for nine years wrote to recommend that I begin smoking cigarettes. "I decided that perhaps nicotine would kill the virus," she said, "and started smoking again on the order of a pack a day. I began to recover and it seems to me that my symptoms worsen when I smoke less." Though she said *it's worth a try,* this was one remedy I decided to pass over. Another woman sent me cassette tapes she recorded on using creative imagery to help me overcome the trauma that must be the underlying cause of my ailment. Her wheezy, rasping voice moved me because of the enormous effort that recording these tapes must have taken.

Another wrote to suggest coffee enemas and full spectrum lights, which, she said, "recharge the looker." She also thought I might benefit from taking a certain immune system modulator which she had gotten from her veterinarian. *Think about it.* A Captain took the time to write from aboard his vessel near Nigeria, recommending a sugar cane rum remedy given to him by a macumba priestess in Brazil. I should take one tablespoon of the concoction after getting up in the morning. Then, he advised, "it might be better to lie down for an hour. It is a mighty powerful drink." He also advised me to brush my teeth when the hour was up. Since alcohol intolerance is strongly associated with Chronic Fatigue Syndrome, I regretfully set this suggestion aside. Another potable cure was recommended by a man who had treated his hepatitis in 1945 with daily draughts of fresh lime juice. When he first got sick, his liver was so swollen that he could feel it pressing against the bottom of his heart and his blood turned the color of urine. Then he found lime. "A virus," he said over the phone, "has a hard time standing up against lime juice." He has had no colds or flu since the end of World War II, his blood pressure is below normal, and his daughter has been on limes since she was weaned. "It was better for her than any vaccine."

According to my notes, by the time the calls and letters tapered off I needed to quit sugar, vinegar, dairy, bread and flour products, corn, caffeine, alcohol and chocolate. Some of these, of course, I also needed to consume in increased amounts. Fruit was out because the worst thing for me was too much acid. Anything that eats outdoors is polluted, so I had to quit meat, fish and fowl. I had to move. I had to sleep both less and more. I needed to have all the fillings removed from my mouth and be cleansed. I needed to see a hair analyst. I needed my head examined. *It's better than nothing.*

There is no doubt in my mind that most of these people contacted me with the best of intentions. Even the independent distributors trying to sell me herbal nutrition products or their unique liquid compound—a secret blending of flowers, foliage, roots and berries of rare botanicals—were probably motivated by a desire to help. There were often blessings; there was deeply felt empathy and an outpouring of personal stories that clutched the heart. Sick people seemed driven to reach out to a fellow sufferer. I came to understand that there is a vast subpopulation of Americans who feel betrayed by the medical community and who seek one another as though they were members of a scattered tribe. Taking matters into their own hands, they are fervent in their outreach, proselytizing like evangelists while expressing their anger at failed bodies and failed expectations of the all-mighty Doctor. "You are a voice in the wilderness crying out," one man wrote, "not for repentance, but a warning that an illness approaches and we need to be called to arms." Revealing myself as sick was tantamount to inviting them all into my life.

Though their calls and letters were meant to be helpful, the cumulative weight of them was staggering. Let me make it clear that I did not go on television requesting advice on how to cure myself. I did not write essays in which I announced my desperation and offered my phone number. Despite the absence of any known drug therapy for Chronic Fatigue Syndrome, I have not reached the end of my faith in Western medical science. Yet the suggestions poured in as though I'd run an ad in the Personals section.

I heard endless variations on the theme of *it's worth thinking about,* often intensified by a version of *desperate straits require desperate measures.* I think these notions all go back to the Father of Medicine, Hippocrates, one of whose aphorisms was: "For extreme diseases extreme strictness of treatment is most efficacious." True enough, but for those with extreme diseases for which there are no treatments, how do you decide which suggestions to try? Certainly drinking a moderate amount of lime juice daily would not hurt me. According to the literature on natural healing, there was something medicinally potent in garlic, in herbs, in certain oils. I had been receiving regular massage therapy since before getting sick. How do you sort the helpful from the hooey, the genuine from the bogus? When nothing your doctor tries to do is of use, how do you define "extreme"? How do you decide when it is time to buy Marlboros and dip the garlic in safflower oil?

◆

I HAD a runty beagle named L.C. who was a great comfort to me in the early years of my illness. Like me, she was shorter than most of her breed and ran with legs churning at a frantic clip; a romantic, she believed in the possibility of true love and conducted her life accordingly. L.C. would jump into my lap to sleep while I lay on the recliner, her chin on my belly, eyes occasionally opening to check me out and see whether I needed anything. I was sure she would get me a glass of lime juice if I asked her to—after all, she could already open the refrigerator to raid it for leftovers. So when I got a letter from a man who signed himself L. C. Young, it seemed like an omen. I ought to listen to what he had to say.

But then, he did not actually want to say what he had to say. L.C. Young was one of the many Inducers, like the garlic man, people whose letters left it up to me to get in touch with them if I truly wanted to get better. They said they had the secret, but the next step was mine and a letter was no place to reveal such information. I might ignore them at my own peril, and generally did. L.C.'s fancy letterhead implied that he had serious scientific knowledge and was connected to a company immersed in study and analysis, though it did not specify of what. The logo, meant to suggest state-of-the-art capability, was of gold-embossed chevrons beside the gyroscopic symbol of an atom with its nucleus being orbited by whirling electrons. He said he'd "been in research some 36 years now and can show you things you dare not print."

He wrote, "I want to offer you the answer to your problem. I ask no fees. I do expect expenses if you want me to drive to your city." Of course, he would be glad to see me in his city too, if that was the way I wanted to handle things.

Another Inducer offered to meet me at his sick daughter's support group meeting and reveal "the miraculous cure that's turned her around." Another wrote to the editor of a magazine in which one of my essays appeared, telling her that his wife had Chronic Fatigue Syndrome too. "I stumbled on a cure that made her well. It has nothing to do with drugs or medicine nor does it involve anything radical; it's just a plain natural method that will restore a person suffering from this problem back to normalcy and good health." I also received a note underneath a comic drawing of Superman gazing out at me, the words "Oh Floyd" floating above his spit-curled head, which said "if you want to correct your imbalance, call me and I will explain what I do." Two people from Manhattan's upper east side, self-confessed "workaholics," wrote to tell me about unnamed practitioners—one a biochemist, the other "not a quack"—both of whom were "very difficult to get an appointment with" and who successfully treated their diseases.

Occasionally contact would come from someone who threatened to be aggressive if I did not do what I was told. In September, as my fourth year of illness was coming to an end, I got a letter from a woman I will call Willa Quincy. She informed me that two years earlier she discovered she had thick blood when she cut her finger and it would not bleed. In an effort to thin her blood, she tried aspirin and vinegar but disliked their side-effects, and was afraid to try salt because of its reputed connection to hypertension. After a year, feeling she had no other options, Willa made "the best choice of her life" and began salting her food. "Now," she said, "when I have an injury I bleed beautifully!" She was convinced that thick blood caused poor circulation, which in turn accounted for the brain abnormalities in my so-called disease, which she felt to be a shameful hoax. Salt deficiency rather than "some non-existent virus" was my problem! Willa also enclosed a letter she had written to the professional golfer Curtis Strange, recommending that he take salt after seeing him complain about his health on television. At the bottom, she noted that he was playing great golf again in Canada and had stated in an interview he felt much better now. She did not say whether he attributed his improvement to salt, though I would be a fool not to see the connection. She also enclosed a copy of a letter she had sent to the national Chronic Fatigue and Immune Dysfunction Syndrome (CFIDS) Association in Charlotte, North Carolina, saying that those of us who spoke for others claiming to have Chronic Fatigue Syndrome had better stop deceiving innocent victims or Willa would have no choice but to intervene. "If you have any moral values, you would notify all of your group leaders about their salt deficiency and assure them that they need not fear dropping dead from high blood pressure if they use salt."

When I did not write back to Willa, she began calling me. I returned from a trip to the Oregon coast to hear her voice on my answering machine.

"Mr. Skloot, pick up the phone," she said. "I took the trouble of writing to you about your health. Now if you're as sick as your article claimed I know you must be there." After a few seconds of silence, and in a voice now resembling a rottweiler's, she said, "Pick it up, I'm calling long-distance!" I could hear her breathing, then growl in exasperation before she turned to someone in the room with her and said "can you imagine the nerve?" before slamming down the phone.

I re-read her letter and was interested to see she had listed symptoms from which salt helped her recover. "To name a few, some are insomnia, lassitude, inability to concentrate, lack of drive, kidney problems, hair loss and personality disorder (hostility)." Maybe it was time for her to increase the daily dosage.

Next time she called, I was expecting to hear from my publisher and answered the phone on the first ring. I had begun screening my calls because of the amount of time unsolicited health-related messages were demanding, but that morning anticipation had gotten the better of my good judgment.

"Why didn't you answer the phone Saturday?" she asked. This was like talking with my mother.

"I appreciate your taking the time to get in touch with me," I said, using my canned speech, "and I'll think about your suggestions."

"Did you try the salt yet?"

"No, Mrs. Quincy, I haven't."

"Well why not?"

"You see, I'm under a doctor's care . . ."

"Did he tell you not to? They all do that, you know, but it's a myth about salt causing high blood pressure. You do what I said and you'll be fine in a week."

"Thank you, Mrs. Quincy. I appreciate . . ."

"And I expect you to write about it too. I want to see you use your gifts to stop this terrible hoax. It's a responsibility you have; you can reach so many people."

"I don't write very much . . ."

"Oh, I get it. You want to be sick, don't you. You like just sitting there collecting your disability and doing nothing all day. I know your kind of man, Mr. Skloot . . ."

I let her go on for another minute or two, inserting an "I appreciate your taking the time" and a "thanks for your interest" here and there. But it was clear she would continue berating me until she got my commitment to become the official voice of the Salt Movement. I hung up on her—politely, of course—and was amazed when she never called or wrote again.

✦

Now I take thirteen and a half pills with breakfast every morning. There is a powerful multi-vitamin, four hefty Vitamin C, an E, a B complex, A and D, Beta-Carotene, two mineral mixes that include Magnesium and Zinc, chelated electrolytes, niacin, enzyme CoQ 10. From time to time, when I see convincing evidence that a remedy was successful in alleviating symptoms like mine, I add it to the cornucopia, regardless of where the suggestion came from. For instance, after a friend in Chicago sent a sheaf of studies, I began taking two tablespoons of flax seed oil followed by a quarter cup of nonfat cottage cheese until the mere sight of the containers in my refrigerator were enough to make me barf. I tried B-12 nasal drops for a while, which oozed bright red into my mustache. I eventually added extra garlic to the menu. For the last year, I have been taking a series of homeopathic remedies.

In 1991, a woman who consumed huge doses of Vitamin C every hour called me from New York to talk about the color of my urine. She described hers in vivid detail, noting that it varied from bright lemon to chartreuse if she was taking too much C but she had learned how to adjust her intake according to the hue. Saffron was no good, I should definitely worry if my urine turned saffron. But amber was fine and so was bisque—a color I simply could not visualize for urine without panic. A man who was tired all the time like me took massive amounts of Vitamin C and was now running marathons again. A woman wrote urging me to go to the Fred Meyers grocery store in her neighborhood and "buy their powdered vitamins plus a book on feet and find what magic will do on your feet."

Then I got a call from Ursula Osnabruck who said that at 54 she cured herself in a few hours. It had been just like I described my illness in the article, even down to losing her curls. Her doctor told her it was menopause. But then she found out the truth: for ten years she took vitamins and that's what made her sick.

"Vitamins rev the motor," Ursula told me.

She and her husband lived on an organic farm, grew all their own food, took wonderful care of themselves. She took vitamins, he did not, and only she got sick. It was because vitamins deplete you of minerals. She stopped taking vitamins and calcium, began taking small amounts of trace minerals, and there was a noticeable change within hours.

"I'm not a crackpot," she whispered. "I'm a member of Mensa."

I did increase my daily dosage of Vitamin C to 4000 mg. But if there is not even consensus about the value of vitamins, how was I supposed to figure out the issue of magnetism? I got more suggestions regarding electro magnetic fields, biomagnetism, and the presence of electronic appliances in my life than on any other topic. We do not yet understand enough about magnetics to grasp how they effect our biological functioning, but it is clear that an association exists. Writing up a prescription for managing it, however, is another matter.

"KICK OFF YOUR SHOES AND GET GROUNDED!!" one man wrote. He said fatigue is a matter of having excess electrical energy in the body, which needs to be grounded in order to get rid of that excess. His advice was to walk outside in the sun, feet bare to the grass, dirt or sand. Sand would be especially good because walking in it builds up the calf muscles. He also recommended deep abdominal breathing while I was outside.

However, being outside, according to several other advisors, would be the death of me. Did I live near a power substation, a microwave tower, electric power lines, radar? Deadly, they said. And indoors was even worse; I was probably besieged by electromagnetic energy with my television, radio, video display terminal, toaster, oven, hair dryer, maybe a home photocopier and fax, an electric blanket in the winter. No doubt I exposed myself to microwaves several times a day too. The only wonder was that I had not gotten sick sooner.

A retired naval officer explained where all the biological and electrical chaos was coming from. Sure there was electromagnetic pollution and excessive reliance on power-driven apparatus, but to believe that was the real problem was to miss the point. Did I not know about the Soviet death grid over America? Was I not aware that they were conducting secret electromagnetic warfare against the United States, destroying our immune systems and mutating our genes and reactivating dormant viruses? There were plenty of reports about this, most of which he sent to me. He also urged me to "study the 13th chapter of Book of Revelations Holy Bible-Christian where this power from heaven is given to Gog-Magog by the Dragon." I might also use the enclosed form to buy a Teslar wrist watch, just the thing to combat electronic smog, and think about wearing a double-ended quartz crystal about my neck.

As a kind of counter-charge to these letters, a man in Portland, Oregon, where I was living at the time, sent a packet of information and offered to sell me the Bio-Magnetic Mattress. Great, I could pay to expose myself to *additional* amounts of magnetic poison. "Heal yourself with nature's energy," he urged. I settled down to read the literature he had sent, but it was difficult because he only included odd-numbered pages. However, I was familiar enough with the work of Robert Becker and Paul Brodeur to know that there were apparent links between electromagnetic pollution and biological malfunction in humans. Given the conflicting reports about electromagnetic fields, I was not convinced buying a Bio-Magnetic Mattress was the solution for me, though it did promise to balance things out. Nor magnetic acupuncture, which the man also suggested. I did, however, buy an extra foam mattress pad to ease the pain in my pelvis.

✦

I TENTATIVELY ventured out of the mainstream. Over the years, I continued trying everything my traditional medical doctors could think to try. There were letters from physicians recommending additional therapies my own physicians had not used and I explored those too. One considered Chronic Fatigue Syndrome a neurotransmitter and chemical imbalance problem complicated by what he called "an overlay of justifiable depression," so he suggested a specific drug I had not used before. Another wrote to say that one of his patients was helped by a duet of antidepressants taken in tiny doses, one at 9 A.M. and the other at 9 P.M. On the other hand, a nurse who had worked in hospitals and physicians' offices for sixteen years wrote to advise me of the limitation of medicine. She said that I should stop worrying about doctors, purge myself of all toxicities and attend a "Sick and Tired Seminar." After all these resources had been exhausted, and after participating without benefit in the Ampligen trial, I turned to the alternative medical world, the naturopaths and homeopaths, the nontraditional practitioners that so many of my unsolicited advisors urged me to consider.

I had gotten an inquiry from a "Counselor and Healer" who said he used "energy balancing," assisting many people to "get in touch with their own healing abilities. He had an offer for me. "Would you be willing to allow me to work on you at no charge? If you receive benefit from the work I do I would appreciate your helping me to edit my book and to assist me by writing some articles when you are strong enough." There were similar calls from two Doctors of Naturopathy, who practiced classical homeopathy as well as food, environmental and chemical allergy desensitization. I finally chose to see a woman recommended to me by someone I had known for many years, a friend who also had Chronic Fatigue Syndrome and swore that Dr. Lucy Forrest helped her.

According to Ted J. Kaptchuk's classic book on Chinese medicine, *The Web that Has No Weaver*, "the Western physician starts with a symptom, then searches for the underlying mechanism—a precise *cause* for a specific *disease*." Although that disease may, like mine, affect various parts or systems of the body, it is viewed as a self-contained phenomenon and diagnosis focuses on "an exact, quantifiable description of a narrow area." Kaptchuk concludes that the physician's logic is analytic, seeking "to isolate one single entity or cause." In contrast, the Chinese medical practitioner looks at the whole individual, body and mind. What is sought is "a pattern of disharmony" that describes "a situation of imbalance" rather than a specific disease or cause. "One does not ask 'What X is causing Y?' but rather, 'What is the relationship between X and Y?'"

I lay on the examining room table looking at charts of the human body decorating the wall. The bodies were criss-crossed by a network of lines and diced into color coded meridians. There was soft, new age music and the lighting was dim. Soon Dr. Lucy Forrest stood at the foot of the table, extended her hand to help me sit, and began asking questions. Her eyes were obviously where all the light in the room had gone. She looked at me more probingly than most Western doctors had touched me. If nothing else, I certainly felt that I had been heard.

She asked me to lay down again and began feeling my pulse for a very long time, nodding, frowning, looking at the charts on her wall. She asked about my body heat, the nature of my sleep, the daily arc of my pain. Then she held a series of small bottles over my chest, saying she was allowing my body to select among the remedies she was considering.

Over the next six weeks, once a week, I came to her for acupuncture treatments and for adjustments in my mix of remedies. I tried a variety of substances with wonderful names—Minor Blue Dragon for my ongoing flu symptoms; Astragalus 10 for immune deficiencies; ground thyroid; Major Four herbs, a sort of ginseng tonic, and something that was the consistency of sand. The acupuncture tended to leave me utterly exhausted and I felt no positive change in my symptoms except when I came to her with a headache, which the needles seemed to shatter like a pane of glass. The various potions also produced no noticeable effect. When I stopped seeing her, Dr. Forrest said I had not given her enough of a chance, which may well be true. But at the time, all I knew was that I seemed to be getting steadily worse and my faith in alternative healing was not yet strong enough to keep me there.

Three years later, I am firmly entrenched in both camps. I seem to have gradually absorbed many of the suggestions my correspondents offered. While seeing my traditional physician once every three months or so, undergoing regular laboratory exams and keeping up with the latest research in drug therapies, I am also considering the most exotic alternative treatment yet: Panchakarma, which is part of India's Ayurvedic, or traditional natural healing system. "Panchakarma," explains Deepak Chopra in his bestselling book *Perfect Health*, is "a systematic treatment for dislodging and flushing toxins from every cell, using the same organs of elimination that the body naturally employs—sweat glands, blood vessels, urinary tract, and intestines."

So it has come to this: Home remedies serve as a kind of mortar between the bricks of Eastern and Western medical practice that provide me shelter during illness. They afford a scaffolding of hope built in large part of material provided by people I have never met, and the growing wisdom to selectively adopt the posture recommended by the Brethren of the Sick around the country (*it's worth a try*).

I am about to embark on a trip to Vancouver, British Columbia, so that I can subject myself to Panchakarma's several steps. I will put out my digestive fires by eating clarified butter; flush my intestinal tract with laxatives; loosen toxins and profoundly relax through the experience of extended massage and the dripping of warm, herbalized sesame oil onto the forehead; rid myself of impurities through herbal steam baths; take enemas to flush out what the other treatments loosen; and inhale medicinal oils or herbs to clear and drain sinuses. If it works, maybe I'll write a letter to someone whose plight I read about in a magazine.

9

Healing Powers

I HAVE NOW been sick for two thousand one hundred and eleven straight days. Not that I am counting, but this is more than fifty thousand hours, over three million minutes, or a little more than one hundred eighty two million seconds.

Ayurvedic medicine says I am sick because my body and spirit are not in harmony. The word Ayurveda means "Life knowledge" and the Ayurvedic system—a 5,000 year old science of healthy living and longevity founded in India—is based on the principle that consciousness, not matter, is primary. What is truly wrong with me is wrong at the level of awareness. I have lost focus and therefore my "quantum mechanical body," cannot keep itself healthy. Chinese medicine says that I am sick because the balance within my body—my *yin* and *yang*—or the balance between my body and environment, is disrupted. My vital energy, my *qi*, which connects me with the vital energy of the universe, is no longer in balance with my blood. Tibetan medicine says that all of us are sick; my disease just happens to be manifest. One of three negative states of mind—desire, hatred or obscuration—has combined with my ignorance of how things exist and what they mean, leading to the present condition of illness. Chiropractic medicine says I am sick because subluxation of the spine has thrown my body into chaos. As a result, I lack normal nerve function. Homeopathic medicine says my disease represents the body's own fight for health. My array of symptoms is merely the wisdom of the body in action, fighting to regain equilibrium, and instead of trying to suppress those symptoms, I should stimulate my body to push them even further. New Age thinking suggests that I am sick because I have forgotten who I am. This caused me to live an unhealthy lifestyle, which in turn made me ill. My illness is a kind of lesson, specifically designed to lead me back to myself. The Bible says that if I am sick, I must have violated stipulations of the covenant with God. Deuteronomy 28 is clear about the source of illness: "If you are not careful to do all the words of this law which are written in this book," the Lord will bring on "extraordinary afflictions, afflictions severe and lasting, and sicknesses grievous and lasting." A corollary biblical explanation holds that my illness is part of undisclosed divine plans. This is something Job came to understand, realizing that "Of a truth, God will not do wickedly." A support group I once attended maintained that we all were sick because we were damaged by our parents or our bosses or environment. We had wounds which festered and finally erupted into illness. A vocal subgroup clarified that we all had similar disease-prone personalities and developed our particular disease because it fit our personality type. And of course my medical doctor says I am sick because on December 7, 1988, a virus targeted my brain and triggered an immune system cascade that my brain cannot turn off. Tests not only trace this path, they confirm the ongoing devastation.

"All our knowledge brings us nearer to our ignorance," T.S. Eliot says in *Choruses from "The Rock."* Indeed, Tom. I have spent nearly seven years reading about illness, learning how the immune and central nervous systems work, understanding how viruses and bacteria and parasites challenge the body, researching drugs and herbs and vitamins, experimenting with the connections between healing and the mind. For all that I have come to know, it seems to me now that the mysteries only grow deeper.

Even without that medley of explanations about the nature of illness to sort through, it is very confusing to be chronically ill. The machine of my body is broken; a delicate poise between body and spirit is disturbed. I have been cut off from my past as an athlete, as a member of the work force, as a vital human being. Family relationships and friendships have altered. Whether I have sinned or lived wrong, expended too much or held too much in, deserved my virus or was stricken arbitrarily, my life has been changed utterly. This is difficult to grasp, even now.

And the messages about how to get well are far more confusing than the messages about what illness is. Let me tell you, sick as long as I have been, you are tempted to try anything.

✦

I DID not used to say I put the milk in the *shower* instead of in the *refrigerator*. I could distinguish between the *excerpts* of Portland and the *outskirts* of Portland. I used to be able to remember people's names after being introduced, or what I came into a room to find. I never used to get lost, but now, without the help of orange ribbons looped around tree limbs, I cannot find my way along a familiar trail through the woods where I live. I peel a cucumber and dispose of its flesh instead of its rind.

In *The Sorcerer's Apprentice*, her brilliant book about medical miracles and life in hospitals, Sallie Tisdale notes that "certain diseases become metaphors, such as cancer or leprosy. They wreak a kind of devastation on the body that seems more than simple-minded cell growth, more than misfortune. They seem to be symbolic of the larger condition, of humanity's changing states." Of course, as Susan Sontag argued in *Illness as Metaphor*, "illness is *not* a metaphor," nor are illnesses "tropes for new attitudes toward the self." She asserts that "nothing is more punitive than to give a disease a meaning" but also realizes that the tendency to do so is "always an index of how much is not understood about the physical terrain of a disease."

Surely both Tisdale and Sontag are right. While my brain is scarred so that lesions are visible on Magnetic Resonance Imaging tests, and the damage to my immune system is readily apparent from laboratory tests, it remains tempting to see Chronic Fatigue Syndrome as somehow symbolic: Our world at the millennium is exhausting. Or it is a hostile place that defeats one's defenses. Or the weak fold; this illness is a perfect example of natural selection at work. Or pushing as hard as most Americans do, we court collapse.

Ultimately, the key issue remains how to balance the quest for understanding my illness with the quest to lead a rich life despite its inexorable presence. Keeping up the with literature, evaluating options, experimenting, but yet not becoming obsessed with treatments and cures, not allowing the stress of such uncertainty to exacerbate symptoms. It is enough to make a person sick.

Try as I might, the temptation to seek strange remedies, to court the healing powers both within and without my body, is often irresistible. In certain moods, I cannot help but see healing as transformation, or feeling that I must somehow reinvent myself in order to get well. When the brain is scarred, when blood flow to it is diminished and functions that were quite literally unconscious suddenly go haywire—like regulating body temperature or remembering to breathe while asleep—a person can grow desperate to get back in balance. When you can neither sit nor lie without pain, or walk without a cane, or sleep through six years of nights, you will consider the most bizarre remedies.

THERE IS a simple prescription for treating one of the newer things to go wrong with me. In his book *Treatment of Disease With Acupuncture*, Dr. James Tin Yau So provides the recipe for a drink that will fix me right up. First, I should obtain a live frog. Next I fill its mouth with whole peppercorns, bind its mouth and legs with thread, wrap it in soft wet clay and put it on a charcoal stove, where it chars until the clay dries and there is no smoke. After the frog cools, I should grind it into a fine powder and place 1/7 ounce of it into one or two tablespoons of wine. Then I must drink it once daily until the symptoms are gone.

I no longer laugh at such suggestions. In fact, I am trying to choose between the frog that lives loudly in our small pond among the water lilies and hyacinths, or the one summering in the heel of Beverly's right Wellington boot on the front porch.

For another set of ongoing problems, there are teas to drink. A mixture of bogbean, black cohosh, celery seed, meadowsweet and yarrow three times a day; then just before bed, a cup of Jamaican dogwood, valerian and passion flower. In addition, I would benefit from wearing Topaz and, from time to time, pearl. Aromatherapy with pennyroyal or peppermint would be very good, as would the use of blue blankets or red tee shirts. Crushed radish juice mixed with a little camphor and taken as nose drops would also help, to say nothing of reviewing the ways I may have violated the Lord's covenant.

I have lain on a table and could have been mistaken for a prickly poppy, with acupuncture needles like erect prickles covering nearly every inch of my body. I have visualized a team of frogmen swimming through my bloodstream to retrain my sluggish natural killer cells in wetwork, and little men in white coveralls scrubbing the lesions from my brain. Every morning I consume a cornucopia of eleven and a quarter different tablets. And of course, I am often tempted to do nothing at all.

That is sometimes offered to me as the soundest advice. Do

nothing. Surrender to your illness in order to defeat it. Stop searching for a cure and be healed. Oddly enough, because medical science does not yet know how to treat my illness, it is the traditional western medical doctor who often recommends doing nothing other than rest and take drugs to alleviate symptoms. A problem with the approach focused on symptoms is the exaggerated impact and side effects drugs have on people with Chronic Fatigue Syndrome. Medications are often taken in minuscule doses, by shaving an eighth of a tablet or opening a capsule to separate its contents into portions the size of a cracker crumb. Still the response might be a complete shutting down of the digestive system, or the sleep of the dead. Another problem is addiction; using drugs for relief of constant pain, sleep disturbance or breathing difficulty carries significant risk while offering little hope of genuine future gain.

So what is a person to do?

In *The Body at War: The Miracle of the Immune System*, Australian immunologist John M. Dwyer devotes an entire chapter to Chronic Fatigue Syndrome in which he berates fellow physicians for their insensitivity and arrogance in handling the disease's mysteries. Failing to get beyond "high technology investigation," they do not consider "medical science's ignorance of so much of the body's ordered and disordered function" and thus do not offer the support their patients need. They dismiss them, ignore them, accuse them of malingering, advise mental health treatment. This has "driven patients with Chronic Fatigue Syndrome and indeed all incurable and poorly understood diseases into the somewhat dangerous world of alternative medicine." With sorrow, Dwyer cites cases of patients who "have flocked to New Zealand to a man who claims to cure Chronic Fatigue Syndrome by exposing one to a specific sequence of colours. Others have been fed massive amounts of vitamin C, tryptophan, lecithin, macrobiotics, cod liver oil, etc. One American healer claims that Chronic Fatigue Syndrome can be cured by tapping repeatedly over the thymus gland and summoning, with all one's mental energy, the T cells that lurk within." Finally, and in a tone of deep despair, Dwyer talks about patients who "go to detoxification units to be purified by enemas, vitamins and exercise."

Well, I tried every one of the remedies on Dwyer's list except thymus tapping. And in June of 1994, Beverly and I drove to Vancouver, British Columbia, to give detoxification therapy a whirl. It made a kind of sense. Even my physician had compared Chronic Fatigue Syndrome to an internal toxic spill, with the immune system dumping its poisons into my bloodstream regularly, so why not clean it up?

◆

THE FIRST step in the detoxification program known as Panchakarma was to be done at home a week before actual treatments began. It was called *sneehana* and involved the consumption of various oils intended to "put out the digestive fire." Beverly cooked up a batch of clarified butter, or *ghee*, which we were to drink in increasing amounts all week, followed by a glass of hot water, till we finished with eight teaspoons on Friday. She said she enjoyed watching it bubble, like a fire flickering, and I was struck by the frenetic sizzling sound, as though the process of purifying butter —and by extension, purifying my body—required a level of intensity and a magic beyond anything I had been working with. For someone with my genetic cholesterol problems, drinking butter was akin to asking a heart-attack patient to run a four-minute mile to strengthen the damaged muscle. It seemed ironic, if not self-destructive, that my detoxification should begin with ingesting something like butter, which I had avoided for the last decade as toxic, but I kept repeating to myself, mantra-like, that this was *clarified* butter.

Each day's increased dosage of *ghee* was a little more difficult to get down, and was followed by slight nausea, but it certainly did diminish my appetite. Beverly, who was going to undergo the same treatments as a preventive rather than curative measure, felt herself being calmed and slowed down.

On the third day, the Panchakarma clinic's director called, just to check on how we were doing and answer any questions we might have. I could not recall my various medical doctors having done that, even after a spinal tap one of them performed on me led to "a neurological event" that left me bedridden for nineteen days.

On the next-to-last day, I found myself deeply fatigued and depressed. Beverly said that the clinic director predicted *ghee* would release old emotions; it was all right, a good sign. That evening, the climax of our preparations, we took hot baths and then consumed six teaspoons of castor oil in a half cup of hot water and the juice of an orange. We held our noses while we drank, then ate a segment of orange to cleanse our palates. I will mention the gurgling in my stomach at bedtime, but not what happened the next morning. Be assured that my digestive tract was cleansed.

Beverly and I had decided to undergo Panchakarma therapy far more circuitously than we make most decisions. After a period of relative equilibrium in the management of my symptoms, the first half of 1994 had seen me worsen notably. My doctor, an infectious disease specialist in whom I have full confidence, had been talking lately about new therapies that were being tried elsewhere—nitroglycerin patches to reverse the restriction of blood flow to the brain, injections of a pig's liver extract, intravenous magnesium—and I found myself hesitant to try another round of experiments. In the past, the experiments had not only failed to help, they often set me back further.

I had been seeing Beverly's naturopathic physician and supplementing my medical doctor's regimen of vitamins, enzymes and supplements with the naturopath's remedies. He gave me tiny white pellets to be taken three times a day without touching them by hand, which is quite a trick for someone with Chronic Fatigue Syndrome. In the quiet evenings here, Beverly and I had been talking about how far I was willing to venture into the medically unknown in order to stop the latest decline.

"Somewhere new," I said.

"What about this?" she asked, handing over the issue of *Yoga Journal*. It was open to an article about Panchakarma, an Ayurvedic practice that she had heard about before. I thought it sounded like a Mexican curry dish, myself.

Panchakarma is aimed at dislodging toxins from cells and flushing them out of the body. It is based on the premise that disease follows from the accumulation of such toxins, and getting rid of them restores the body's proper balance. Every avenue of egress from the body is used, but it is supposed to be a gentle, soothing process. After being cleansed, a person goes home to work on the forces that allowed the toxins to build up in the first place—behaviors, particularly dietary, which are antithetical to the particular body type a person is born with.

I read the article, then the chapter on Panchakarma in Deepak Chopra's *Perfect Health*, and we sent away for brochures from a half dozen clinics offering the treatment. The world of Ayurvedic medicine is as alien to me as space/time travel, but I thought the literature sounded convincing enough to give it a try, despite the scoffing in Dr. Dwyer's book. Although the settings, accommodations and trappings varied widely, the actual detoxification routines were fairly similar. So instead of paying $2,850 plus air fair to Iowa for a week-long residential package, or about $1,600 for a five day sojourn in New Mexico, or driving all the way to the Santa Cruz area, we opted for Vancouver, a six-hour drive from home, a city we both enjoy visiting.

The clinic occupied the upstairs unit of a townhouse in a quiet residential neighborhood on Vancouver's south side. I was glad the area seemed clean and friendly, because with no sign on the street or the door, it felt less like visiting a clinic than a bookie.

Inside, the furnishings were spare—two bedrooms used as treatment rooms and containing only a padded table for the patient, in the living room a futon that faced a long table where only a telephone sat, a bathroom, a kitchen where the various oils and herbal potions were concocted, and behind a folding Japanese screen in the dining area, a computer and fax machine hummed.

Our first visit was for a Sunday evening conference with the clinic's director and medical doctor. The doctor would briefly examine us and outline our specific treatment plans. She had a separate, "regular" practice in family medicine and was working with the Panchakarma clinic out of her personal belief in the value of Ayurveda. After a lengthy round of questions about my health, my diet and my lifestyle, and a three-minute reading of my pulse, she asked whether I was a person who meditated.

"I haven't had much luck with that," I said.

She looked at the clinic director and frowned. "I can't work with people who don't meditate. I just can't relate to them."

She prescribed a series of treatments for me over the next five afternoons, involving oil rubs, the dripping of warm oil onto the center of my forehead, herbalized steam treatments, a kind of full-body oil bath, daily enemas, inhalation of various oil and herbal mixtures, and music. Despite my preparatory reading, I was beginning to feel strongly as though I were trapped inside a film by Federico Fellini. The best surreal art is rooted in recognizable reality and this was a real room, the staff looked as conservative as the merchants I had seen downtown, everyone was smiling encouragingly, but I was having trouble seeing this plan as something to heal and rejuvenate rather than punish me.

We were staying at an isolated Bed and Breakfast overlooking English Bay, a good ten miles from the city's hurlyburly, so that we could spend leisurely mornings and evenings resting between treatments. Our room, whose wall-wide window crept up to serve also as half a roof, gave a remarkable view of woods, sea and sky. Basic, elemental stuff as we lay there gazing at the stars, purifying ourselves, and yet by Tuesday night I was miserable. The mixture of summery heat and gallons of hot oil conspired with my body's inability to regulate its temperature, making me horribly uncomfortable. I could not tolerate the herbal steam treatment at its target heat level, which meant that I received a sort of luke-steam session. My eyes, already preternaturally dry, were ready to be reduced to powder if I had to put my face over a bowl of medicated vapors. The enemas seemed to trigger some deep, unacknowledged phobia, leaving me so stressed that I could barely sleep. I was not enjoying wearing a diaper all night, either. Everything that bothered me was proclaimed to be a good sign by the clinic director, indications that the treatment was working. Beverly, meanwhile, felt wonderful and could not wait for the next day's treatment. Clearly, as she quietly reminded me, I needed to make a choice: quit or surrender to the program. "A massage and an enema," she said. "What's the big deal?"

I was a classic case of a person whose mind and body are working at cross purposes in the healing process. Here were these people trying to unleash my body's own healing powers and I was hindering them by using symptom warfare. Did I not trust them or the process enough? Did I want to stay sick? Well, no. That's why I'm spending all this cash. But I felt as though the treatment was worse than the illness, and would end up worsening it. Nevertheless, I vowed to practice discipline the next day, to turn my body over to them and take my mind elsewhere. That was the day the enema tube, on being withdrawn, scratched my insides badly enough to make further enemas impossible, which was not a good sign.

By the end of a week, despite the enema escapade, I had undergone most of the prescribed treatments, at nearly the prescribed levels of intensity and for close to the recommended amounts of time. I left Vancouver having experienced a simplified Panchakarma, a sort of Cliff's Notes version, and returned to Oregon with a recommended program of home care and diet, anxious to see what effect the experience would have. We were warned that it might take one to three months before we could fully assess the benefits.

✦

I SUPPOSE if I were Forrest Gump, I might approach the end of this essay by saying "healing is as healing does." Because healing seems to me to be a phenomenon that involves action, however passive that action may appear to be. It is possible to rest aggressively. It is possible to empty oneself of thought, especially negative thought, or to train the mind to turn away from its experience of pain, and thereby experience a lessening of that pain. The very act of doing something perceived as potentially beneficial has certain healing consequences, whether or not the thing done is of any demonstrable value—this is the placebo effect and its efficacy can be substantial.

Through all the years of my illness, through the many traditional and nontraditional efforts I have made to get better, I have developed deep respect for the paradoxes and possibilities of the body's healing powers, even if I have not been able to marshal them all on my own behalf. My symptoms wax and wane, sometimes, it seems, as a result of my efforts and sometimes despite them. Nevertheless, there will be times, however brief, when I am able to function with a nearly clear mind for hours at a time, or run a few steps up to the mailbox to see whether something I have written has found favor with an editor. I danced with Beverly at our wedding sixteen months ago, and though I am not sure if the enzyme supplement CoQ 10 I was taking had anything to do with it, I am still taking the stuff.

It is now September, 1994, and I must say that a number of strange changes have developed over the three months since my experience with Panchakarma. Almost immediately, I began to sleep through the night for the first time since the winter of 1988.

Did Panchakarma do this for me? I had a brief period of slightly more stamina, during which I was able to walk for a half hour at a time and write for as much as three hours during the day. My cholesterol went down twenty points, but there has been no change in the profile of my overactive immune system. However, my joint and muscle pain have increased enormously. The first signs of arthritis manifested themselves in my feet and hands, and headaches have put a stop to all activity for days at a time. I developed asthma. I developed a case of pityriasis rosea, an inflammatory skin disease common among young adults that left me covered in scaly lesions from thighs to chest for two months and for which my doctors have no explanation. They think it may have been a reactivation of an infection I caught and defended myself from in childhood, but which my damaged immune system could no longer subdue. Could Panchakarma have had anything to do with these new problems? Do I have to go back and try it again to find out?

I have neither lost my respect for the paradoxes and possibilities of the body's healing powers nor figured them out well enough to make use of them. I have not yet worked out a master theory on why I got sick or a master plan on how to get well. But as the contradictions deepen, as what works and what does not work develops its own strange rhythm, I feel as though I have learned to approach the dance of hope and despair with high style. A maturing expert in the healing fandango, I have achieved a state of mind that allows me to accommodate its variations, to risk the odd step for the sake of the song. That alone seems like growth.

PART FOUR

The Elements of Happiness

"What poor elements are our happinesses made of, if time, time which we can scarce consider to be any thing, be an essential part of our happiness!"

—John Donne, from "Devotions XIV"

10

Out of Time

Illness & Writing

"Poets make long poems to contain what they have learned and to set the parts of their knowledge in order."

—Donald Hall, from "Text as Test"

THERE IS SOMETHING I've been wondering about ever since the morning of December 7, 1988, when I woke up sick in that hotel room across the street from The White House. I mean, it is an unstable enough world, and back then the Evil Empire was still in existence, so the idea wasn't that farfetched. Besides, I have read enough fiction by Ross Thomas or John Le Carre to know these things happen with impunity. What I wondered is whether The White House, which Ronald Reagan was about to leave for George Bush, had anything to do with it.

Stranger thoughts have worked their way to the surface. On the very morning I got sick, it occurred to me that I might be changing species because I could smell the odors of everyone who had ever stayed in that hotel room, could hear the snow that would begin falling later that day, and could taste in the room's air a spice I had never heard of or tasted before, something I believed was called *frumiac*. Then when I could not lift back the bedcovers because they had become so heavy while I slept, I suddenly understood that I'd been transported overnight to the surface of Mars.

It would be six months before I could read something as complex as a recipe, a year before I could write anything coherent again, two years before I could sit erect in an auditorium long enough to hear a symphony, three years before I could walk for thirty minutes at a time. You should see me try to figure out how to reassemble the two pieces of my poultry shears after washing them. I still can't get through a day without at least one period of lengthy sleep and several of complete inactivity. There are long periods when thirty minute walks are only a memory.

During those first years, I was in there the whole time; I was experiencing and sensing and feeling—eventually even thinking— but all I could do was store things up. It was a kind of enforced accumulation of knowing, and when I began to write again, a few minutes a day on a good day, it no longer seemed possible to write as I had written before.

✦

IN THE fall of 1915, without money to support the continuation of her New York art studies, Georgia O'Keefe impulsively agreed to teach at Columbia College in South Carolina. I like to imagine the scene. This was the year Margaret Sanger was jailed for writing the first book on birth control; the nation's idea of femininity had a lot to do with Theda Bara and those feline, titillating moves known as vamping which she first revealed in the 1915 film *A Fool There Was*. At the time, Columbia College, just outside the state capital, was essentially a Methodist-operated finishing school. Georgia O'Keefe was twenty-eight, unknown, had not yet exhibited her work in public. But she was already a radical artist, a highly independent woman, in turmoil about her art, her relationships, and her sexuality. She was just beginning to paint flowers in the characteristic O'Keefe manner, and earlier that year was stirred by having read *Women as World Builders*, a popular study of feminism by Floyd Dell which affirmed her own feelings that "the woman who finds her work will find her love."

Of course O'Keefe felt terribly out of place and alienated at Columbia College. Columbia was not unlike Amarillo, Texas, where she had hidden herself for two years beginning in 1912, or New Mexico, where she spent most of her life after 1929—isolated, remote, almost outside of time. Which was just what she needed in order to achieve major advances in her work. She wrote from South Carolina to her friend Anita Pollitzer back in New York, saying she was uncovering "things in my head that are not like what anyone has taught me—shapes and ideas so near to me—so natural to my way of being."

During the Thanksgiving holiday in 1915, O'Keefe was visited at Columbia by Arthur Macmahon. The two had met and grown close the summer before in Virginia, where the O'Keefes had a rooming house in Charlottesville and where she could attend summer school at the university. In his 1992 biography *O'Keefe: The Life of an American Legend*, Jeffrey Hogrefe, who apparently knows every detail about the sexual encounters in her life, reveals that O'Keefe and Macmahon were lovers for the first time during this visit. Shortly after Macmahon left she had a breakthrough in her work. "She had found her talent: an ability to interpret psycho-sexual landscape in a way with which millions of other people could identify." Hogrefe says that O'Keefe "recorded her impressions as a clairvoyant receives messages from the other world. The act was as spontaneous as it was frightening: there on the paper was her soul in a horrific mass of lines and forms."

Coming into her true subject matter and form in these 1915 drawings, O'Keefe wrote to Pollitzer: "Did you ever have something to say and feel as if the whole side of the wall wouldn't be big enough to say it on?"

This episode moves me deeply. You never know where your

breakthrough is going to come from, or what will make it necessary for you to work on a much larger scale than before. But I've come to believe it has much to do with isolation and removal, with a break from time and from customary life. Like living in the hinterlands, like the sudden incursion of passion, chronic illness certainly provides such a break, a place where you are lost out of time, where your life is interrupted and you are turned inward deeply.

✦

IT IS difficult not to see the lesions on my brain as lesions in my *self.* My balance, my long- and short-term memory, abstract reasoning, concentration, and coordination remain shot. The pupils of my eyes don't dilate and contract properly, so being in bright light is painful. The *flight or fight* response is not functioning properly so my body handles any kind of stress inappropriately, failing to release the right level of hormones along its pituitary-adrenal axis. Seeing a tense movie can make my lymph nodes swell and my hips ache. Recently I watched a muscle-toning videotape with Beverly, trying to mimic the minimal exercises being shown—we're not talking frantic aerobics here—listening to instructions offered over light background music while a half dozen figures facing me on the screen twisted and flexed in the direction opposite to the one being suggested by the leader. I was unable to move, though Beverly floated through the routine without a hitch.

In conversation, and in the initial stages of composition when I write, I often cannot locate words that are in my vocabulary. Consequently there are either lengthy pauses while I search for a word or I become a walking encyclopedia of malapropisms, given to calling the curtains my wife made "windshields" and calling Christmas stocking-stuffers "pot stickers." Close, but wrong, as though my brain had been hotwired by Norm Crosby.

As a writer, I've been changed utterly by illness. On my best days, I can work for two hours, total. It can take six months to produce what once took a week. Though I've used my computer and WordPerfect software for a decade, there's no telling what I may do when I reach for the function keys, which adds a new wrinkle to the idea of venturing into the unknown with one's writing. I can no longer approach my material—a poem, an essay, a story, certainly nothing as ambitious as a novel—with a meaningful overview. Instead, I must work from bits and pieces, first finding *whether* and then finding *how* things I'm working with fit together. Composition has become much more a matter of patience, of waiting and yielding the will. It's as though the very impulse to write has altered and, in many ways, the idea of what a poem is has changed. While there is still the desire to capture moments of intense emotion, to explore a specific memory or sensation, there is more often the realization that I need to keep the poem open, that more is contained within what I might perceive as the moment. I keep hearing a sentence from Ezra Pound's *Canto II* echoing and falling back over itself: "I have seen what I have seen." It has come to mean for me more than simply "I've witnessed a lot." It also means "I have examined the things I witnessed and learned from them."

Finding form for a piece of work has become an obsession because I can no longer justify having assumptions about how things cohere. Though some of my poems may still rhyme or have traditional structure, and some may tell a story, there are often fractures within that structure and the shapes feel very fluid to me, inclusive rather than exclusive. The idea of resonant conclusions, of wrapping up, is growing more strange to me. I like to let the process of composition go on a little longer, to add things, to reroute. In some ways, I don't recognize my writing any more. I am reminded of how it felt, during the one week in the past twenty-four years that I had my beard shaved off, not to recognize the reflection I saw in windows and mirrors as I passed by.

Perhaps even more significant has been the way illness has changed my relationship to time. For the last five years, I have lived out of time almost entirely. Especially in the early years of my illness, it was nothing for me to sleep all day and be awake all night. Because I am disabled and cannot work, my days and weeks have a shape that does not adhere to the traditional work day or week. I cannot ignore how my body feels, or my level of exhaustion, and so might nap twice a day—at ten and again at two—for two hours at a time. As Kathy Charmaz points out in her book *Good Days Bad Days: The Self in Chronic Illness and Time*, "If someone does not improve, things look and feel quite differently. The slowing of time continues. Chronology blurs." Strangely enough, I've come to see my disjunction with the traditional concept of time as liberating and vital to what little writing I can do. I've also come to see it as a metaphor for the mindset that permits the writing of long poems. Charmaz notes that "Losing the regularity of clock-time can allow for greater depth of thought." This is more than a fancy way of putting the old cliché that illness gives you a chance to reassess your priorities. Charmaz reports the case of a chronically ill patient for whom "being immersed in a stretched-out duration of illness had permitted her unexpected spiritual discovery and development" and concludes that "as illness continues, most people lose ways of shaping and giving meaning to their days." The same idea is raised by Dr. Oliver Sacks in his remarkable book, *Without a Leg to Stand On*, which concerns his experience of becoming a patient after sustaining a severe leg injury: "I have since had a deeper sense of the horror and wonder which lurk behind life and which are concealed, as it were, behind the usual surface of health."

I'm not saying that you have to be sick to write a long poem, though the thought did occur to me ten pages into one poem I wrote about a group of young hikers lost during a storm on Oregon's Mt. Hood. Without wanting to overstate the case, I'd like to suggest that when poets turn away from the traditional, timebound, short lyric toward the longer dramatic or narrative poem, something similar goes on with respect to time, to discovery, to ways of shaping and giving meaning to experience. New ways of shaping and giving meaning to material develop. Things open up which are concealed behind the usual surface of the shorter poem.

◆

VALERY SAID that poetry is to prose as dancing is to walking. Before getting sick, I might have used this analogy to further suggest that the long poem is to the lyric as a marathon is to a sprint.

In the marathon, as I recall, you don't simply find a comfortable pace and settle into it for the duration. The race is filled with discrete challenges you must plan for and adjust to—changes in terrain, changes in wind direction or intensity, the buildup of heat, the problem of taking nourishment or the moment of remarkable discomfort when your body stops burning carbohydrates and switches to burning fats. The graph of effort does not map evenly, the marathon's rhythm is not steady. As a 26.2 mile race, it may have a beginning, middle (at 13.1 miles) and end structurally, but it has another rhythm entirely within that structure. It's quite common to hear runners say the middle of a marathon occurs at the twentieth mile. I remember the marathon as a very inclusive event in which a runner monitors everything that's going on inside and out. Except perhaps for the elite runner or the runner on a mission, the successful marathon occurs outside time, in a dimension where to finish well you heed the requirements of your whole system—body and mind—despite time. A sprint, however, is a sustained explosion of effort. To be successful, it will be sustained at the maximum level possible from start to finish. Focused and exclusive, ignoring everything extraneous to the moment, it is all about time, about forgetting the body and controlling the mind long enough to finish fast.

Since getting sick, I would make a different analogy, one that now feels a bit more accurate. The long poem is to the lyric as lengthy illnesses such as Multiple Sclerosis, Lupus, Rheumatoid Arthritis or Chronic Fatigue Syndrome are to the flu. Lengthy illness isolates people, turns them inward, makes them reconsider identity. As Kathy Charmaz suggests in her writings about the self in chronic illness and time, "ill people wonder where illness will take them and ask who they can be during their odyssey." Illness not only gives them the context but eventually demands that they do such wondering. I'm glad she used the word *odyssey* because that sense of extended journey is important to understanding the illness experience as well as the ways in which it approximates the experience of writing a long poem. It's also the title of a fine long poem itself.

Illness conflates time. The past with its memories and the future with its altered imaginings mingle with present sensations and experience to create the sort of gumbo that is both the heart of wonder and the perfect culture in which a long poem can grow.

◆

IN 1969 and 1970, when I studied with Thomas Kinsella, I was just twenty-two and knew exactly what I wanted. The master would show me his tricks and I would write poems about my dead father and yearning for love that stunned people with their emotional power. Kinsella had begun teaching at Southern Illinois University in Carbondale four years earlier. I moved there from New York, arriving in the fall, that time of year Kinsella later described in a memorable stanza:

> The lake water lifted a little and fell
> doped and dreamy in the late heat.
> The air at lung temperature—like the end of the world:

a butterfly panted with dull scarlet wings
on the mud by the reeds, the tracks
of small animals softening along the edge,
a child's foot-prints, out too far . . .

I should have been prepared for strangeness.

Kinsella's reputation had been built on tight, elegant lyrics such as "Another September," "Fifth Sunday After Easter," "The Secret Garden," or that harrowing twelve-line thriller of mist and loss called "Tara." He wrote short, self-focused poems that were above all orderly and accomplished, often exquisite ("April's sweet hand in the margins betrayed/ Her character in late cursive daffodils;/ A gauche mark, but beautiful: a maid."). They showed a tormented poet stark naked in the glen of his suffering and I loved them. Although one poem, "Baggot Street Deserta," stretched for eighty lines—a rigorously focused, late night meditation on memory and the act of writing—virtually everything else was compact and bursting with what the critic Calvin Bedient has called "subdued but unrelenting power."

The marvelous anthology piece "Mirror in February" was my favorite Kinsella poem, with its vivid first stanza showing the poet doing just what I thought a poet ought to do, look at himself:

The day dawns with scent of must and rain,
Of opened soil, dark trees, dry bedroom air.
Under the fading lamp, half dressed—my brain
Idling on some compulsive fantasy—
I towel my shaven lip and stop, and stare,
Riveted by a dark exhausted eye,
A dry downturning mouth.

I wanted to write like this, which is why I went to study with him. But Kinsella didn't want to write like this. Not any more.

He had just published a collection in America called *Nightwalker and Other Poems*, which included both the 400-line title poem and the 225-line "Phoenix Park," along with a 161-line poem called "The Shoals Returning," a 134-line poem called "A Country Walk," and "Downstream," which was only 83 lines long. I was out of the country when this book appeared and didn't know it existed. Almost nothing rhymed anymore. Most of the poems were less *arranged*, more open. They were interior to the point of being almost subterranean, yet they included more of the outside world than ever before. Even "Phoenix Park," with its rigidly controlled eleven-syllable lines and five-line stanzas, was bulky with external matters, weird associational leaps, departures both literal and figurative. Things welled up and demanded to be included in poems that would have ruled them out before. History, politics, literary reference. The poems teemed.

I didn't know what hit me. When I met with him, we would talk about such poems as D.H. Lawrence's "Autumn at Taos," Robert Creeley's "The Finger" or Austin Clarke's "Ancient Lights" and Kinsella would praise them in ways that suggested he actually liked such works. Man, they not only didn't rhyme, they weren't tight; they *leaked*.

Kinsella was moving toward a poetry in which, he has said, nothing should come between the poet and his material, between perceiving self and the things perceived. No inherited forms, no imposed structure, no real endings or beginnings. "I have never seen," Kinsella said in a 1986 interview with John F. Deane, editor of Dublin's Dedalus Press, "why a poem need end absolutely with its final line. It can lie in wait, with the dynamics available." I heard him say something similar in 1969, wrote it down in my notebook, read it over when I got back to my apartment and thought, 'Maybe it's not too late to transfer.' I'm glad I stayed.

Those ten- and fifteen-page poems Kinsella wrote at mid-career were to look like short ones compared with the book-length sequences such as *Notes from the Land of the Dead* and *One*, or twenty-five and thirty-page poems like *St. Catherine's Clock* and *A Technical Supplement* that he was to write over the next quarter century. Like Ezra Pound, Kinsella has in many ways been writing one long, ongoing poem since 1965 or so, an exploration of "how the whole thing works."

Kinsella was forty-one when I met him, the same age I was when I got sick. He was in self-imposed exile after a twenty-year civil service career in Ireland's Ministry of Finance, living outside the framework of his entire previous adult life, and clearly on a journey. He was turning his back on everything that had brought his work acclaim. He was rejecting the imposition of order. Instead, as he later said, "I believe the significant work begins in eliciting order from actuality." He also has commented that "It is out of ourselves and our wills that the chaos came, and out of ourselves that some order will have to be constructed." For Kinsella, this meant abandoning such traditional ordering devices as meter and rhyme, then narrative, eventually even rejecting beginnings and endings. Everything came from within; nothing was imposed between the poet and his material. Sitting at his desk, pen in hand:

> The key, though I hardly knew it,
> already in my fist.
> Falling. Mind darkening.
> Toward a ring of mouths.
> Flushed.
> Time, distance,
> meaning nothing.
> No matter.

It must also be noted that this was 1969-70, a time of great turmoil and tearing down of existing structures. Kinsella was hardly the only poet born in the late Twenties, coming to full maturity in the late Sixties, who rejected traditional forms and turned inward. But he was virtually the only one to turn almost exclusively to the long poem for his exploration of all he knows, all he is, all he comes from.

In His essay "The Poetic Principle," Edgar Allan Poe declared, "I hold that a long poem does not exist. I maintain that the phrase 'a long poem' is simply a flat contradiction in terms."

Poe believed that it was impossible to write a long poem. As he said in another essay, "The Philosophy of Composition," he thought that any composition masquerading as a long poem was in truth "merely a succession of brief ones," a string of intense poetical effects held together by prose—by narrative or meditation or characterization—even if the prose happened to look like poetry. *Paradise Lost?* "At least one half prose."

His logic was clear enough. Poe thought that a poem was a poem "only inasmuch as it intensely excites, by elevating, the soul." Since through physical necessity intense excitements are always brief, he felt it was literally impossible to sustain such writing for long.

Poor guy. Of course, we in the late twentieth-century know that intense excitement can be sustained for great lengths of time. The Pulitzer Prize and National Book Award winning writer Richard Rhodes recently published a book called *Making Love: An Erotic Odyssey*, in which he devotes an entire chapter to research on extending sexual orgasm ("would you believe four hours?"). It is fun to imagine how Poe, who wrote "Annabel Lee" about "this maiden there lived with no other thought/Than to love and be loved by me," would react to four-hour orgasms. We also know about the endorphin high brought on by long distance running, a level of pleasure that can sustain an exhausted marathoner through an hour or more of performance. Or consider meditation. Certainly one purpose of meditation is to extend the intense moments of stillness, those initially brief flashes which eventually can be made to last for great periods of time. According to Sogyal Rinpoche in *The Tibetan Book Living and Dying*, "you will discover for yourself that there is a gap between each thought. When the past thought is past, and the future thought not yet arisen, you will always find a gap in which the *Rigpa*, the nature of mind, is revealed. So the work of meditation is to allow thoughts to slow down, to make that gap become more and more apparent."

It might be simple to dismiss Poe's contention that a long poem is a contradiction in terms by saying that his definition of a poem is too limited. Or to say that if a long poem doesn't sustain a high level of excitement, so what? Why must we bring the critical criteria by which we judge short poems to bear on long ones? But I also think Poe's notion of the boundaries of intense excitement is suspect. At any rate, his point is essentially structural—he believes the connective tissue holding together a long poem's more highly charged moments dissipates that charge. It is not clear why they cannot work as well to intensify each subsequent charge, building the poem to an overall greater level of power the way some lovers vary their rhythm or use other techniques to delay climax. Or why the connective components of a long poem cannot offer a different kind of quickening, like an Adagio in a symphony.

Perhaps Poe's opinions were colored by his personal situation —the wretched childhood, his parents' and wife's early deaths, his health, his failures and penury and grief—which was hardly conducive to sustained work. Perhaps it was colored by his peculiar blend of romantic nihilism. At any rate, he wrote only fifty poems or so, devoting most of his literary energies to money-making stories or journalistic efforts, and neither his material nor his approach to it invited the kind of breadth that justifies a longer poem.

However, not only is the long poem possible, I believe it is unavoidable for certain material or certain frames of mind. It was clearly impossible for Ezra Pound, who believed he knew everything and saw how everything connected, to consider writing shorter poems once he found himself at work on his *Cantos*. To understand the long poem as merely a succession of intense poetical effects is to misunderstand the impulse to gather and make sense of the world that distinguishes such work from its shorter, more lyrical kin.

✦

In conclusion, I would like to consider two pieces composed by Franz Schubert. In 1817, when Schubert was twenty, he composed *Die Forelle*. This small song was based on a poem about a trout swimming in a clear stream, written by Christian Daniel Schubart. The trout, whimsical and capricious ("launische"), is able to avoid being caught until the fisherman bewilders him by muddying the water.

Schubert entirely omitted the poem's conclusion, a stern moral which warned young women to avoid the seducer with his fishing rod ("Verfuhrer mit der Angel"). Instead, he concluded his song simply with the catching of the trout. He was after charm and whimsy, not moral lessons. And the song's brief format was not intended to extend consideration beyond the moment between fish and angler; there was no room in it for the author and his commentary.

Two years later Schubert used his trout song in the fourth movement of his brilliant Piano Quintet in A, also known as "The Trout Quintet." Here his original whimsical tune is used as the subject of a seven-and-a-half-minute set of variations that is itself part of a much longer whole. The old theme and its new variations, which are at the heart of Schubert's Quintet, led him to produce an extended piece that not only captures the original's melodious radiance and warmth, but enriches it vastly. Now there is room for more than the encounter between fish and angler. In the amplitude of a longer work, there is sweetness, to be sure, loving duets in the strings, gently flowing passages for the piano, frolicsome melodies. But there is also moroseness, hectic interludes, sudden shifts in character that shatter the calm. There is danger, a sense of the way caprice doesn't only suggest whimsy but also suggests the arbitrary power of the unknown, perhaps of a capricious God, though the music's delightfulness always seems to assert itself again.

I love both *Die Forelle* and the Piano Quintet in A. I listen to both, in different moods, and return to both for enrichment. Of course, I can appreciate the argument that music can do what poetry cannot, can accommodate the longer work in ways that poetry does not. But I don't buy it.

The long poem thrives today, despite the critical commonplace that says it is in trouble. Perhaps in our fragmented, alienated world, it must thrive for us to find connections, to assert order. My poetry library here in my small writing room—even after having moved three times since 1990, even after The Great Book Giveaway of 1991—is packed with contemporary long poems in journals, individual collections and anthologies. Ai, John Ashbery, Neal Bowers, Carolyn Forche, Dana Gioia, Patricia Goedicke, Albert Goldbarth, Jorie Graham, Donald Hall, Seamus Heaney, Lynda Hull, Mark Jarman, Thomas Kinsella, Kenneth Koch, J.D. McClatchy, Robert McDowell, Gary Miranda, John Montague, Robert Pinsky, Dave Smith, Charles Wright. Even Floyd Skloot.

11

Thorns into Feathers

Coping with Chronic Illness

"As thou hast made these feathers thorns, in the sharpness of this sickness, so, Lord, make these thorns feathers again."

—John Donne, from "Devotions III"

IN THE WINTER of 1623, the great English poet and preacher John Donne was stricken with epidemic typhus. "Variable, and therefore miserable condition of man!" he wrote. "This minute I was well, and am ill, this minute." Typhus, a louse-borne bacterial disease, killed hundreds of thousands throughout Jacobean England. Donne at age 52 suddenly found himself feverish, tormented by headaches, covered with spots. He took to his bed, where he felt "my slack sinews are iron fetters, and those thin sheets iron doors upon me." Not only were those sheets transformed into iron doors, the feathers of his bed had become thorns. The situation was alarming enough that King James's own physician was dispatched to Donne's bedside.

The course of Donne's illness was summarized in 1640 by his biographer, Sir Izaak Walton: "God preserved his spirit, and kept his intellectuals as clear and perfect as when that sickness first seized his body; but it continued long, and threatened him with death, which he dreaded not." One enduring outcome of Donne's typhus episode was the writing of a brilliant book, *Devotions Upon Emergent Occasions*, a 17th-century best-seller in which he mused passionately on the condition of his stricken body and soul. In what is perhaps the mother of all blurbs, Izaak Walton said the *Devotions* was "a book that may not unfitly be called a Sacred Picture of Spiritual Ecstasies."

Thinking about coping with my own long-term illness, I find myself drawn in particular to Donne's third Devotion. Lying in his feather bed, which fever and pain transform into a bed of thorns, he asks God to reverse the alchemy and turn his bed back to feathers. Now in my own illness, I am sorry to say, God has not seen fit to keep my intellectuals as clear and perfect as when sickness first seized me, but I believe I have found the secret of that alchemy Donne prayed for. I have taken matters into my own hands and, if I have not exactly turned the thorns of my illness to feathers, I did find ways to soften their spikes.

✦

IF YOU knew me five years ago, before I got sick, you would not know me now. Some of it is style, of course, or style reflecting substance. Cannot run anymore, so in place of the running gear in my closet I have a hazelwood cane bought in Rapallo, Italy, during my honeymoon. Cannot work, so there is a wardrobe of baggy sweats or wildly patterned, floppy pants instead of the trim three-piece suits and shirts with snug collars. Look down and there are clogs instead of wing-tips, since for years it was a challenge just to tie my shoelaces. I wear a small hematite ball in my left earlobe now and use fingers instead of a brush to manage my hair, which—like my beard—is shot with gray. Though it is no heavier, the lean and hard body that I worked so diligently to sculpt is much softer now. As my wife Beverly says, it seems like my armor is gone.

But it is more than style. A lifelong city boy, I now live in the country and love it, despite the spiders and carpenter ants, despite skunks and the occasional porcupine, despite poison oak or a well that threatened to go dry and its iron-rich water that stained me amber. And I am slow now. I used to move through my world like a halfback, cutting sharply, zigging and zagging, always trying for that extra yard, very difficult to bring down. Now I conserve, I loiter, I move as in a dream; because if I don't, I will either fall or smack into something. But of this necessity has come a whole new way of being in my life. This goes for talking too, which I do at a more leisurely pace, interspersed now with actual listening. Something different and vital has emerged. My secret is that I have found the places within me that illness could not touch. I have learned to honor them.

Take music, for instance. Before I got sick, music to me was late fifties and early sixties rock & roll. Give me doo-wop and Top 40 AM, Elvis and the Everly Brothers, Buddy and Fats and Chuck and Jerry Lee. Give me Girl Groups and The Four Seasons, and throw in a little Broadway show music for variety— Guys and Dolls, Flower Drum Song, Camelot, South Pacific. Music was for singing along with the phonograph, or with headphones if I had to jog through downtown Portland because winter mornings were too dark on the wooded trails of Forest Park. As background to dinner, or when company arrived, there was light jazz to show my extreme sophistication.

This was music. Obviously, it was not the stuff for listening to all day while lying in the bed or recliner month after month. This was not the proper stuff for a brain riddled with anatomic holes, for a mind so easily confused by stimuli that I could not drive or sit in a restaurant unless I faced the wall, for a body that needed to rest and heal. In my illness, I did not need the Wall of Sound.

One day Eric, my best friend and running partner, showed up with some Mozart. He brought Schumann and Schubert, a Beethoven piano sonata, Bach. Who?

"Nothing heavy," he said. "No symphonies or anything complicated."

I did not know what he was talking about. Classical music was by definition complicated and heavy, I thought, which was why it was discussed in hushed tones and pompous accents. It was written by people without first names, most of whom were cranky and tubercular and had wild hair. Not that I was a philistine; after all, I do have a couple of degrees with honors in literature. I have read all of Thomas Hardy, even *The Hand of Ethelberta*, and I pick up T.S. Eliot or Robert Lowell for sheer pleasure. But classical music had somehow remained outside my experience.

Eric sat with me and listened to the music, mostly solo piano, or piano with violin, and one or two chamber pieces. As he said, nothing complicated. He pointed out a few things, but mostly just sat there across the room from me with his eyes closed and listened. After a few days, he brought over something he said was a little more complex; if I did not like it, I could just go back to flute and harp. When I heard the first melancholy notes of the cello in Schumann's A-minor Concerto, my world changed. I did not know much about classical music, but I knew the music of illness when I heard it.

I probably averaged four hours a day supine and surrounded by classical music during the first two years of my illness. It was not all sweetness and light: sometimes music took me to the very center of my experience, to the conflicts I was feeling about all that had changed in my life, the vortex of emotions. But sometimes it took me outside myself altogether, into a realm of pure sound, where there could be peace. Once, Eric called to say he would take me to buy a book on music appreciation. By the time he arrived at my door, half an hour later, I had not only forgotten he was coming, I did not even recognize him. He nodded and we sat down to listen to Chopin, who was a lot sicker than me for much of his life, before heading to the store.

Without what music taught me I might not have known how

to grasp that the score my body had followed for life was totally rewritten. I would not have taken into myself the knowledge that my body's symphony now included a long movement of pure chaos, somber and discordant, but one that would lead somewhere worth going if I learned to listen.

This was a deep, intuitive way to understand what my illness does to the body, throwing its intricately balanced, complex systems into disarray so that nothing works as expected anymore, a cacophony of symptoms. Music has taught me my being could still contain harmony, if I could only hear the whole thing through.

✦

OR TAKE time. I have come to see that it is entirely possible to do just that, to *take* time, to seize control of it rather than be controlled by it. Paradoxically, the way to take control of time is to let it go altogether.

Often alone, I experienced the timelessness of solitude, the way everything slows down long enough to speed up while a person is immersed in illness. Though John Donne says, in his fifth Devotion, that "as sickness is the greatest misery, so the greatest misery of sickness is solitude," I did not find this to be true for me. Solitude became a kind of chamber in which my separation from time and the world of measured change made sense. Because I was removed from the world of work—meetings, lunches, schedules, deadlines—outside the familiar rhythm of a traditional day, I soon found that a week's very shape was lost. Time goes by so slowly (yes, rock & roll lyrics still seep through). Days drag, it is impossible to believe how long a day really lasts, but then I look around and all of a sudden it is autumn, and where did the time go?

Soon I learned to eat when I was hungry and sleep when I was tired. It is not that appetite changes in chronic illness, it is that being chronically ill provides an opportunity to become aware of appetite and how it works. I found that I did not have to eat three meals a day, or eat at fixed times. I could graze all day long if I wanted to, or eat twice a day, have waffles or an omelette (with fake eggs) in the evening or a chicken pot pie in the morning. I found myself approaching sleep the same way I approached food: grazing. I napped for a couple of hours in the late morning and again in the mid-afternoon because that was when I was too tired to be awake. It was how my body managed the illness.

Finally, I weaned myself from the constant measuring of the slow changes that accompany chronic illness. I gave up the thrice-daily graphing of my body temperature (mine was subnormal, the two-year graph reflecting minute fluctuations from 97 to 98.2) and the ongoing compilation of weekly sleep totals. I stopped weighing myself every morning. Oddly enough, all these changes did was provide me with a sense of greater control. "What poor elements are our happinesses made of," Donne writes in his fourteenth Devotion, "if time, time which we can scarce consider to be any thing, be an essential part of our happiness!" The man certainly had a point.

None of this—the sense of disjunction with time, of learning about my body and its appetites—should have been surprising to me, but it was. Before getting sick, I would have said that as a serious competitive runner I was a person who knew my body and its needs. That was why I was running, to help body and soul deal with working full-time and being a parent to my children and the family's chief cook and writing for a couple of hours every night. Time was a matter of being where I had to be when I had to be there; it was a matter of pace and records to beat. Before a 10 K race I would be doing my stretches in a group with runners who, like me, planned to race at 5:40 per mile, and we would babble about the condition of every tendon, every muscle, the little bones and frail ligaments, fast and slow twitch fibers. Good runners, the books and magazines said, listened to their bodies; I was certainly one of those listeners. Baloney. Perhaps if I had paid attention to what my body was saying, I might have understood its message in time.

So time, and the way my body functioned in time, turned out to be something I did not understand until getting sick. Time turns out to be a truly inner phenomenon. Despite clocks and agendas and appointments, regardless of records and goals, setting aside calendars, time was in fact a measure of how I experienced my self moving through my life. I began to look at my illness in a new way: it had not taken time away from me, it had given time back to me.

✦

THEN THERE is love. I am talking about passionate, intense, erotic love, the kind of connection that seems impossible when someone is seriously and chronically ill. The kind that comes from so deep inside, the place seems to have been closed off by illness. Or worse, poisoned by it.

Sick people often feel that such love is simply impossible anymore. It seems so difficult to sustain if they are married and sick, living day in and day out with the illness always there between them. Finding new love is beyond imagining if they are single and ill, requiring a level of effort as inconceivable as competing in a decathlon. If truly fortunate, they might have something else in their lives, perhaps a supportive, nurturing love, familiar and comfortable, that becomes romance's version of the sick-bed: a safe place in which to rest, to convalesce, to take care.

Being sick, feeling so weakened and out-of-it, I was no longer the person who knew himself capable of passion's true eloquence. I felt as removed from it as from the rest of my old life's defining activities. So I was simply astonished when passion found its way to the dry places inside me, when it anointed them and I knew myself touched where I had given up hope of ever being touched again. Then astonishment was replaced by the understanding that I must act on what I felt, that I could and must respond to the erotic feelings I was capable of having. Not that I could suddenly run a marathon again, or spell and do math reliably; not that I could remember birthdates, or walk without a cane, or get through a day without at least one long nap. Of course I could not miraculously function as though my central nervous system and immune system were normal again. But I found that Eros is a remarkably restorative force, life-affirming and optimistic.

So is touch. For years before we married, Beverly was my massage therapist, coming to my house every other week, lugging her portable massage table up the staircase, setting it up in my living room, and bringing me the healing power of touch. We were never intimate in the sense of being lovers then; Beverly is not a woman who would ever compromise her professional ethics. But we became close friends through those years—me lying there with my eyes closed, the sheets smelling of sweet almond oil, Beverly moving around me for an hour with her powerful hands, her resonant voice becoming familiar as a recurring dream while we spoke softly to one another about our lives. There were times when my joints and bones were so tender that her touch nearly jolted me from the table, but we found a way to manage that pain and bring ease to my body. I think we built a connection based on shared openness, on the sonorousness of intimate conversation.

"The disease hath established a kingdom," Donne writes in his tenth Devotion, "an empire in me." It often seems to those who live there that passion has been banished from the land. Curiously, I found it locked in the Emperor's own dungeon and together with Beverly set it free.

◆

FOR ALL they take away, chronic pain and illness also bring opportunity. The great challenge is to cope, but coping may not mean what people initially think it means.

The word "cope" comes from the Latin for "strike" or "blow." It implies activity, not passivity, engagement rather than withdrawal. I think it is among our signal responsibilities to accept the opportunities illness brings us and do something with them. That is how we cope, fighting back at the diseases which challenge us.

In his great seventeenth Devotion, the one in which a church bell tolling softly to commemorate someone else's death also tolls for Donne, the author says "affliction is a treasure, and scarce any man hath enough of it." Well, I cannot say that I agree with him there, don't give me that business about this being some kind of prize. But I am with him fully when he goes on to say "No man hath affliction enough that is not matured and ripened by it."

Now I live in a round house Beverly built in the middle of twenty hilly acres above a small town called Amity. How appropriate that the word *Amity* means 'peaceful relations,' since this is the place where I have found the peace that is part of converting the thorns of illness into feathers. Amity is in wine country and our closest neighbor on the hill is the gifted vintner Keith Orr, who owns and operates Tempest Winery from the white metal building on his property. From the room where I write, I see the pond that Beverly dug amidst Douglas fir, maple, wild cherry and scrub oak. Heavy, flat stones that she carried out of the woods, lugged through the blackberry vines, and used to shape the pond's edge are now ringed with brush to keep deer away. Otherwise, the deer would eat all our water lilies and hyacinths, fifty-dollar snacks, and would knock the stones into the water while leaning down to drink, tearing apart the pond liner. One of the cats—plump, queenly Zola, who looks far too equable to be the fierce hunter—has just sashayed past the window, a mouse dangling from her mouth. Two adirondack chairs scream *spring will come! spring will come!* while tilting rakishly back toward a sun that has not yet burned through the winter fog. Beverly bought and painted them magenta eighteen months ago, on that first weekend she brought me out here from Portland.

I am not saying that listening to music, modifying eating and sleeping habits, loving, and moving to the country will give control of a life taken over by illness and pain. For each person, surely, the details will vary, the untouched places will be different. But finding the places within that illness cannot reach, and learning to honor them, can help transform the bed of thorns that is illness.

12

The Comeback

Phase One: The Collection

I STARTED MY comeback modestly enough. At the time, I was thinking about Robert F. Murphy's *The Body Silent,* an account of his journey into the world of the disabled, in which he says "You are just as alive as you always were, and what are you going to do about it?" So in the winter of 1991, as I neared the age of forty-four, I phoned "Manny's Baseball Land" in New York City and ordered myself a 1955 Brooklyn Dodgers baseball cap.

Long-term, chronic illness is a series of forfeitures and recla-mations. Work, sunlight, travel, restaurants, alcohol, parties, the-ater were all impossibilities. Possibilities took shape eventually: appreciating impressionist landscapes or the sound of a viola from the confines of my cushioned recliner, talking on the phone with other people who were ill, writing about my experience. Coffee and black tea were out; I came to appreciate camomile or blackberry tea. In place of sugar-laden breakfast cereals or cookies, I learned about those sweetened with fruit juice. Transformation became a word I could take seriously. In this way, the idea for a baseball comeback began to form.

My new old Dodgers cap was beautiful, the proper shade of royal blue with a classic white Brooklyn 'B' and button, but its long bill and high-crowned contemporary style seemed all wrong. The caps I remember from my Brooklyn childhood were more rounded when new and crushed across the crown when properly broken in. They were part of the head, not adornment. My new cap made me look like a pretender, a tax attorney wearing his pin-striped yellow bell-bottoms and a brown leather vest on the weekends to show he'd been there through the crazy years. But I had truly seen the Boys of Summer in their prime at Ebbets Field. I could remember the very look not only of Reese fielding grounders, Snider coiled at bat, Robinson sliding into home, and Furillo throwing a rocket from right, but even of George Shuba shooting a liner into the gap, Karl Spooner in his one year of pitching glory, and back-up first baseman Frank Kellert, who turned thirty-one the same day I turned eight and thus was practically family. For me, it was an act of reclamation to wear my new cap in the shower, to sit on it while I watched a televised baseball game, to subject it to the blazing August sun that is always a surprise here, or to fold it up into a tube shape and stuff it in my back pocket.

My cap became a rumpled masterpiece. But one was not enough. In the spring of 1992, I added a 1917 NY Giants cap— John McGraw's team, that ethnic, pennant-winning hash comprised of stalwarts such as Benny Kauff, Union Man Holke, Slim Sallee, and an aging Heine Zimmerman. It was two sizes too small, but those glorious old caps, modelled after the type used by cyclists and jockeys, were supposed to be worn back on the head a bit, pointed slightly upwards. They should look jaunty and I was at a stage of my illness where a little jaunty was good. Besides, since I was not about to be running anywhere and seldom went out in a strong wind, an exact fit hardly mattered. However, style mattered, and casting a snazzy shadow when I hit a few fungoes with a pine cone ball and my hazelwood cane bat. So I made it known to Beverly that my classic cap collection had begun and soon had a 1911 NY Yankees cap as well. My bookcase now held one cap from each of the old New York teams.

Phase Two: California Dreaming

By the summer of 1993, four and a half years after first getting sick, I was ready to risk a short journey. At first, I did not realize it was part of my baseball comeback. Beverly and I drove down to northern California, where I was to be a writer-in-residence at the Villa Montalvo in Saratoga for six weeks. At that time I could write for about two hours on a good day and my project while there was to work on essays about the illness experience.

Since we were not supposed to arrive at the Villa until the morning of July 1, we checked into a motel near Fairfield late on the afternoon of June 30. Within a half mile of the motel there was a baseball batting range, which I had spotted from the highway only seconds before realizing it was time to find a place to stay for the night. Good thing I'd brought my caps.

Though I still used a cane and my balance was uncertain, I could walk three times a week for about an hour, but was still totally disabled. More than the hyperactive immune system, more than the muscle and joint pain, sleep disturbance or constant exhaustion, it was the neurological complications that made daily life a challenge. My legs and shoulders were always bruised from walking into furniture or walls that I saw perfectly well. I hated it when I put my tea in the refrigerator and pressed the handle to heat it up, or could not figure out how to slip a pillowcase on properly, or could not write a phone number down correctly.

As we approached the batting cages, I heard the strange sound of balls plinking against aluminum bats. A young man in cut-off jeans and a tank top was driving himself crazy popping every pitch into the nets above home plate. Well, perhaps we might show him a thing or two about the line drive. At the attendant's booth, I rested my cane across the window ledge while hefting a few bats. The young woman inside the booth did not seem to think this was strange. She shoved five dollars worth of tokens at me and shook her head as I tugged down my Giants cap.

"What's wrong?"

She reached back for a batting helmet. "You have to wear this. Insurance says. We don't want anything to happen to your head."

"It's a little late for that."

I was demoralized. Instead of looking like Bedford Bill Rariden, I resembled a little leaguer in my oversized, generic plastic helmet, droopy socks, and a strap tee shirt that was so big on me the underarms were tucked into my shorts. Still, this was no time for excuses and besides, I could swear that I heard Beverly, under her breath, singing "The National Anthem." Although it had been twenty-seven years since I last swung at a pitched baseball, I somehow felt sure that if conditions were right, I would have lost little. I adjusted the helmet. One thing was certain: bat in hand, I had forgotten I was sick.

Now, as we strolled down past the fifty- and sixty-mile an hour cages toward something appropriately challenging, it was time for me to tell Beverly about that last game of baseball back in 1966. Because either I had not told her yet, in the one year we'd been together, or somehow she had forgotten all the details.

It was a cold Thursday in May and I was a freshman at Franklin & Marshall College. Although now F&M is a power-house in Division III competition, ranked ninth in the country in 1995, when I played there we were a truly ragtag bunch. In my freshman team photograph, the seventeen of us sport three different styles of uniform, half of us wear thick eyeglasses, and all but a few appear to be thinking about the chemistry labs they were missing. I am in the front row with the four other guys under 5'6". I remember that our entire season had been rained out, every game, and we were making them all up in a two-week blitz of double headers. This game, the finale against Elizabethtown College, was tied. In the last inning, with one out and a runner on third, an easy fly was hit to me in short left field. I could see the runner come back to third in order to tag up and was astonished—I mean, I was close enough to him to see that his neck was ringed with dirt. He was out at home by twenty feet. Of course, since this is both my memory (which is, I admit, notoriously compromised by illness) and my final game of organized baseball, I was the first batter up to start the extra inning. I hit a double to right-center. I stole third. I was given the signal to steal home as well and took off on the first pitch. But the batter, a brilliant philosophy student from Massachusetts who was already well-known for his erudite skepticism, either did not catch the signal or could not believe it was true. When he started his swing, I was less than fifteen feet away and dove for his ankles like a free safety. My final personal baseball memory is of the four of us—me, the batter who had fouled the ball off, the catcher and the umpire all tumbling into the backstop.

Clearly, as comebacks go, I did not have far to travel despite my physical limitations. But they say a person should set manageable goals in the recovery process; all I wanted to do at this point was hit a pitched ball. Earlier, I said that I could no more hit a fastball than I could fly; now it was time to test that assertion. Beverly stood behind the cage, fingers gripping the chain links, short blonde hair peeking out from under my cap, and called encouragement. Batting righthanded, I stuck my butt out and assumed the old crouched stance, waiting for the machine's arm to come up. But of course this was 1992 and pitching machines no longer have arms, just holes about where a pitcher's throat should be, blinking lights, and suddenly a fast ball sizzled past me chest high. My swing was so late the next pitch was about to be released when I straightened myself out. The helmet, of course, was now on sideways.

Then, for a period that lasted less than ten minutes, everything clicked. I swung easily and scattered line drives all around the range. Every fifteen pitches, Beverly would open the screaky cage door, step in behind me and drop another token in. I would switch sides of the plate and continue swatting liners like Wade Boggs or Paul Molitor. But as suddenly as it had arrived, the magic passed. My aluminum bat weighed twenty pounds and my swing became jerky. Blisters blossomed on my thumbs and palms. Mercifully—because I would have stood there swinging until I collapsed—at the end of the round of balls, there was no creaking of the gate behind me, no clinking of a token into the slot. Bless Beverly's heart. When I turned around, she was smiling at me, claiming to be out of tokens, her voice full of love.

About two weeks later, after we had settled into our routines at the Villa Montalvo, Beverly and I drove to Santa Cruz for a Friday night at the Boardwalk. I had recovered from my exertions in the batting cage, was writing for two hours most mornings while Beverly painted, sleeping through the afternoons, and enjoying the comradeship of my four fellow artists-in-residence. But it was terribly hot, near one hundred degrees every relentless afternoon. Since one of the systems affected by my illness is the autonomic nervous system and I can no longer regulate body temperature, I desperately needed to be where it was cooler.

As we strolled arm-in-arm along the Boardwalk, we came to a booth where stuffed animals could be won by throwing baseballs at metal bottles and knocking all six off a table. Certainly the balls were soft, as though ground chuck had been sewn under their leather covers, the bottles were heavy as brass, and the tables were rimmed to discourage bottles from rolling off. You had to blast the bottles off with a Sandy Koufax fastball, hoping the ball itself did not simply splat when it hit them. No problem.

It never crossed my mind to consider that I hadn't thrown a baseball in ages, or that my inflamed joints might resist a motion which can ruin even a well-trained young shoulder. But I was here with my sweetheart, there were stuffed pink elephants all over the wall, the evening was sparkling under the Boardwalk lights and the sound of the surf was more or less like the cheers of a crowd. The ball I threw first came so close to knocking an elephant off the wall that the barker must have thought I misunderstood the rules. No, sir, you hit the bottles and then I hand you the stuffed animal. The second ball smacked the table front and bounced off to one side, not even sending a shimmer up through the bottles.

Beverly has the most infectious laugh. When she lets loose at one of my fiction readings, it always brings the audience along with her—the perfect set-up artist. The sound she was making now, though, was more like a gasp and I knew she was trying to hold her laugh in. Time to get down to business. My last throw hit the bottles dead center; four actually flew off the table, a fifth rolled off without hesitation, but the sixth turned back from the edge as though for a second run and quit with its top hanging over the rim.

The barker, no doubt fearing that I would stick around and win his largest prize, gave me a small stuffed Dalmatian with ears like a bunny and wished me a good night. The puppy carries a bow in her mouth on which is written, in quaint cursive, "I Love You." She is named Lucille and has a place of honor on the bedroom bookshelf.

Phase Three: Second-Hand Balls

One of the most frustrating aspects of long-term, chronic illness is the confusion created by relapses. Do I feel better today, hasn't this been a fairly good week, and might that mean I am in fact recovering? A brief period of improvement sometimes may extend itself toward true remission, then suddenly turn back. Was it something I did? The trip to Seattle for a reading, the twenty-minute walk after not being able to walk at all for months, the lamb chops, the vacuuming? Was it the new nutritional supplement that costs $43 per month, or the new unscented underarm deodorant? Perhaps it was something I did not do, the afternoon nap I skipped or the flax seed oil I stopped taking because it gagged me and did not seem to be helping. Maybe I should not have had that operation on the tumor in my foot just yet, or should not have taken the pain medication those three post-op days, or the trip to New York so soon afterwards. Every decision is freighted with such consequence. But somehow I knew that it was necessary now to include baseball in the treatment program.

Amity, the small rural town at the bottom of the hill, is an old German settlement halfway between Portland and the Pacific coast. Its population is 1,100 and we are well outside the city limits, in what I think of as suburban Amity, though we can hear the cheers from Friday night football games at the high school as they rise up around us. In downtown Amity, the bank, the gas station and the video rental shop have closed. The only photocopy machine in town, which had been housed in the hardware store before *it* closed, was moved over to Dad's Market, where we can conveniently buy small-town goods at big city prices, and where it broke down weekly until being sold off last year. The two cafes don't close, they just become other cafes every year or so. Forfeitures and reclamations. The bank is about to open up as an art gallery, the gas station houses a used car lot, and the video rental shop is now, of all things, a realtor's office. But there are four enduring second-hand stores in Amity. North to south, the main street's three-block-long commercial area offers Michele's Antiques and Second Hand, located in a former hamburger hut, the Amity Second Hand, which seems always to have been the Amity Second Hand, the Amity Old and New in the Cronk

Building, the only building with a name built into its facade, and—just before you cross ash swale—The Litter Box, a former residence whose porch has a hand-painted sign offering Free Cloths.

One Saturday morning in the spring of 1994, Beverly and I went downtown to see if we could find a baseball and two used mitts for playing catch beside our vegetable garden. This would be spring training, because by now, after more than six years of illness, my comeback had been given serious form by my publisher, Story Line Press. Robert McDowell, Story Line's publisher, had quietly been encouraging my efforts for several years. Since I had never told him about my comeback, his encouragement was even more miraculous. When Beverly and I had gotten married, he gave us a brand new baseball inscribed "From Story Line Press" and signed by the entire staff, all four of them. For years, we had been exchanging baseball memories, old baseball cards (I actually gave him my 1953 Preacher Roe card!) and baseball book recommendations. When I told him about my exploits in California he said, "Good, we can use you."

Based in a small town near Eugene, Oregon, Story Line had put together a team in the Mens' Senior Baseball League. Players in the league, who ranged in age from thirty to over sixty, included several former minor leaguers, a former all-pro offensive end for the New England Patriots, one-time semi-pro players and refugees from summer softball leagues. Story Line's team, officially known as the Dodgers but affectionately dubbed The Story Line Nine, was comprised mostly of poets, novelists, publishing professionals, and a few friends or siblings who—in other contexts—could be thought of as "ringers." Their expectations were, I think, more aesthetic than competitive: let's play this lovely game with integrity and respect, let's make it rhyme, and let's look good. I had an open invitation to come and join them for one of their Sunday doubleheaders, to be a Designated Hitter if I could not play the field, to take it easy and have fun. Little did Robert know that his friendly, charitable invitation had spurred me toward the climax of my comeback.

By now my cap collection included a 1938 Brooklyn Dodgers, which looks like a blue and white parakeet cage with a 'B' where the door should be, and a 1920's New York Yankees, an imposing dark blue job with no contrasting button and only its shiny white NY to disturb the stark simplicity. This, the hat of Ruth and Gehrig, was not a hat to mess around with, and I only wear it on weekend mornings—before my shower—when my hair is mussed from sleep. So my cap collection was growing, and I had visited another batting range near Portland—with equally encouraging results and with even more blisters—but the comeback was static. I could go on adding caps, I could swat balls in a cage, but unless I could find my way to a new level of baseball involvement, it would all become dilettantish. To put it another way, I was at a safe level of baseball and needed to push the envelope, to see what was out there. I would get ready to play, if only for an inning, for the Dodgers.

We found two used baseballs in the Amity Second Hand. They were the same shade of gray as my 1911 NY Yankees cap, worn and scuffed but still stitched tight, and we bought them both because our field of play was bordered by poison oak and a stupendous drop-off toward the valley below. But the only mitt was for a child of five, too small even for my hand, and we were forced to drive fifteen miles into McMinnville to see what K-Mart had to offer. We debated whether to buy one or two mitts, since living on only my disability payments limits our discretionary spending. Beverly could wear it and I would catch her throws barehanded. But no, this was almost a pharmaceutical purchase and we felt we had to do it right—generic brands, perhaps, but full strength—even if Met Life wouldn't reimburse us. Beverly liked the Kirby Puckett model; I liked the Joe Carter, which resembled a jai alai cesta, had a web larger than the entire mitt I used in college, and cost $24. Hanging on a rack nearby, on sale for one week only, were an assortment of batting gloves. I remembered the blisters, dredged up the Medically Necessary argument, and we got one, for the left hand, in Dodger blue and white.

Softened by mink oil, ball nestled in the pockets, the new mitts lay on our living room credenza for a week while it rained and the creek on our property ran wild. Then, caps in place, beaming, we went outside in the midday sun to toss a ball around. I was a very happy man.

Phase Four: Rhapsody in Dodger Blue

We drove the two hours to Eugene on an August Sunday morning and when we pulled into the parking lot beside the school, I had a moment of grave indecision. Should I leave my cane in the truck? I did not want to fall on my way to the field, which was a long walk from the parking lot, but if I could not walk that far how could I expect to bat? To run, if the occasion warranted, or play the field if things got that far? However, leaving the truck without it felt terrible; I brought the cane for later, for after the game, just in case I needed it after all my exertions.

When we arrived, I could not believe my eyes. The game was about to begin! We had gotten started a bit late, and the drive took a bit longer than we had estimated, and batting practice was over. This meant that if I did play, I would be facing my first live pitching in twenty eight years during the game, cold. It occurred to me that if the pitcher threw a curve ball, which the pitching machines I had faced lately did not, I might faint as it broke across the plate.

Robert McDowell greeted me with a hug and directed me to the grocery bag at the end of the team's bench. Inside was a gorgeous, accurate Dodgers uniform, blue and white with a red number 32—Sandy Koufax, who was a great pitcher but, with an

.097 lifetime batting average, one of the worst hitters ever to play the game. Good thing I had brought my red Converse high-top sneakers.

I shook hands all around, played catch with teammates, even tried jogging across the outfield, ninety feet at a time. Beverly, seated in a beach chair near home plate, waved her 1938 Brooklyn Dodgers cap. It occurred to me that I could be bed-ridden for the next month after this escapade. Big deal.

The rules allowed each player to bat, regardless of whether he was playing the field, and we had twelve men to get through before my turn came. Our opponents, the Rockies, were in first place and we were in last place, and there were very salient reasons for both of those situations. They had a great team, with a left-handed pitcher capable of throwing in the mid-eighties, and we could not buy a hit. As the thirteenth hitter in the Dodgers lineup, I got to bat once in the seven inning game.

We have three photographs to prove this actually happened, that it was not a figment of a sick person's active dream life. The first photograph shows me smiling at Beverly from the on-deck circle instead of studying the pitcher's delivery. Batting glove in place, helmet and sunglasses in place, I have the bat resting on my shoulder and I look unutterably cool. You can tell it is me, though, by the glowing white patches in my beard. Next to me, a teammate with his ponytail resting atop the number 8 on his back, does study the pitcher. The next picture shows me, good old number 32, framed by chain link as I waggle the bat menacingly. My feet are pointed toward that 315 foot sign in right and no one in the picture looks sick. In the final picture, I am crouched in the batter's box and the pitcher is at the top of his windup. It's the same stance as from my college days, butt stuck out, elbows up, still and calm. The viewer's eyes automatically gravitate to the red, high-top sneakers.

It is the perfect frozen moment in any person's comeback. Nothing has happened yet; everything looks ideal. I was here, doing this, even though now, a full year later, I cannot take my daily walks and am grateful if I can spend two hours in a day working on this essay.

Before striking out (on a bad full-count call, I must add), I did manage to foul a fast ball over the backstop behind home plate. Robert still compliments me on my level, powerful swing. In game two, I came up to bat against a right-handed pitcher and by then was so exhausted and befuddled that I forgot to hit lefty and did nearly fall over trying to follow his curveball with my eyes.

There was still one more thing to do. As the time grew later and the score more lopsided, a few teammates had to leave for other Sunday obligations. Having sat in the dugout for more than three hours, except for my two trips to bat, I volunteered to play an inning at second base. Robert, after asking whether I was sure, sent me in.

Neurologists use a Romberg test to determine whether a patient's postural sense is deranged, whether he can stand up without relying on his eyes to identify his place in space and maintain balance. In this test, the eyes are shut, the arms are extended, and the patient tries to stand with feet together. This is also what happens when a second baseman drifts back toward shallow right center under a pop fly, gets a bead on it and spreads his arms, looking up, calling "I got it." Like the Romberg test, this is something I cannot do. I collapsed, landing flat on my back as the ball bounced beside my face. I heard Beverly's scream before I could sit up.

None of this felt like failure. It was hugely embarrassing, to be sure, since I was careful to assure that my reputation as a college player had preceded me. However, nothing was riding on my catching that pop fly or getting a hit because we were so soundly defeated in both games, and my teammates were most gracious—or perhaps simply glad to see me trot off the field before I committed any further errors.

I am through playing for the Dodgers, though I will certainly accept Robert's invitation to watch them play this summer. But I feel as though I reached an important turning point in the management of my illness during that phase of my comeback. Playing baseball is clearly beyond me, but my love of the game continues, I am writing about it, I have rented a satellite dish in order to watch major league games, and the cap collection has moved off into bold new territory. I just bought a St. Louis Browns cap; it's the kind that the 3' 7" Eddie Gaedel was wearing when he pinch hit for the Brownies against Detroit in 1951, and that one-armed Pete Gray wore when he played a season for them during World War II. My 48th birthday is next week and a suspiciously light package arrived for Beverly in last week's mail, about the size and shape for something containing a baseball cap. Maybe an old Phillies cap, or a St. Louis Cardinals, something red.

Baseball, the way I remember and embellish it, has room for all sorts of strangeness, for a midget and an outfielder you would have sworn was disabled, for star outfielders like Babe Herman, who managed to take a fly ball smack on his 1920s Brooklyn Dodger cap. It has room for me and I certainly have room for it. I have reclaimed something that had been lost to illness. The comeback continues.

The Art of Illness

WEBER IN LONDON, SPRING 1826

"I am now a broken machine."

—Carl Maria Von Weber (1786-1826)

I want to be home before my breath gives
out. I want to see Lina and my son.
Dear God, I must breathe in the sweet Dresden
air, warm and dry in June. A man who lives
for music dies into the same silence
as one who lives for God or sword. My work
is done. There is nothing beyond the dark
to fear, nothing to lose. The opulence
of oblivion seems heaven to me
as my feet swell, my hands shake and I reek.
I am the color of wheat. Lifeblood leaks
from me everywhere and now I can see
sleep is no use. It is time for me to
begin the journey. I came here to earn
money for my family but I yearn
for one thing only. Bring me home to you.

"To be a genius, as this man plainly was, and have
something beautiful in you and not be able to rid
yourself of it because you could no longer see your
score paper and no longer hold your pen—well, the
thought was unbearable!"

—Eric Fenby, from *Delius As I Knew Him*

Always toward sunset Delius grew
restless and uneasy in his carriage
chair, raving at the pain in his legs,
flicking his long tapering fingers
as though stating a theme on the air.
His proud head, pale as marble,
began to wobble no matter the effort
to hold it still. He demanded a thick
rug for warmth. He demanded a thin rug
for comfort, then demanded that no
rug touch him, all the time wanting
me to read one more story aloud
like a child refusing to go to bed.

Delius required that everything
be just so. His bean and barley
soup must be salted in the pot
and served piping hot. No rattling
cups or clattering spoons at table,
where chitchat lashed him to fury.
After dinner, one cigar and a slow
push up the Marlotte road in silence,
when even the neighbor's great Alsatians
walked hushed beside us. Saturdays
we could play only Sir Thomas Beecham's

records of Delius on the gramophone
in the quiet of his music room.

One morning in the faded garden
where Delius sat beneath the elder
tree, I could see that he was angry
with me. Tossing his head from side
to side, he champed and glared
toward the rising sun, clearing
his throat *fortissimo*. At night
a melody had come on the verge
of sleep, making him weep to be
hearing new music leap in his mind
again. But I overslept beneath
the full-sized face of mad Strindberg
by Munch, dreaming myself south
to Paris amidst a wild summer storm,
surrounded by young friends in good
health, rain playing a sudden cadenza
on the swollen Somme and the thunder
in E-Flat. I wanted tea.

My hair still damp, my face creased
by sleep, I took up paper and pen
without a word. I sat cross-legged
on the grass wondering whether Delius
would sing to me. Would he call out
the notes and their time-values?
At last I was to do what I had come
from Scarborough to do and free him
of the music. He threw his head
back like a wild horse in flight
and neighed toneless to the sky.
"Hold it!" he said, causing me

to drop my pen, then he bayed
toward heaven again. I heard
neither words nor notes, only
a shapeless cry. He could not
bring forth the tune he heard!
Dazed, all I could say was
"Delius, what key is it in?"
"A minor, Fenby, don't be slow."

Fingers inky, spectacles blurred
by tears, I confess being blind
as Delius himself when I groped
for the sanctuary of his porch.
Of course, in time we learned
to bring forth his music, imagining
ourselves on cliffs in the heather
looking out over the sea, knowing
chords in the high strings were
a clear sky. But I shall never
forget Delius, a shrunken relic,
mouth opened in anguish, gripped
by the awful beauty inside him.

RAVEL AT SWIM

"The inability to communicate speech, writing or
music when the peripheral nervous system is largely
undamaged is called an aphasia."

—John O'Shea, from "Maurice Ravel:
Aspects of Musical Perception"

Something dark has stolen the sea from me.
Always a seal in water, I found its
melodies and swam open harmony
through them. Now I flail. Nothing I do fits

the rhythms around me. *Swiss Watchmaker*
they called me for the design of my work.
Mere lover of wind-up toys, a baker
of sweets, as though elegance were a quirk.

Now the hand that holds forks by their tines floats
like driftwood on the sea of music spread
before me. It will not write down the notes
I hear like a gull's bent tones in my head.

It will not play what I see on paper
and know I wrote two years ago to be
performed one-handed. (That was a caper!
I loved having such limits placed on me.)

It will not sign my name. It tries to light
a match with the tip of a cigarette.
What is left? It took me eight days to write
a fifty-six word letter I have yet

to end, consoling a friend whose mother
just died. I do not want to be seen now

by anyone who knew me at another
time. Pure artifice, they said, missing how

my need for form affirmed the passions of
my heart. They must not see me with the link
from brain to limb severed and all I love
lost. Sheer formlessness surrounds me. I think

but cannot share my thoughts. I remember
every flower's fragrance, the taste of lamb
roasted for hours over charcoal embers
at summer bazaars, lips on mine, but am

powerless to express myself. Let me
be alone. Let me have the grace of pure
music in my head, where I hear and see
perfectly. That silence I can endure.

BEHIND GERSHWIN'S EYES

"Nobody else smelled burning garbage because
Gershwin's olfactory sensation came from a slow-
growing tumor on the right temporal lobe of his
brain."

—Joan Peyser, from *The Memory of All That*

They did not believe him.
They told him the smell
of burning garbage was all
in his head. Some mornings
it was all he could do
to lift his head from
the pillow. Some nights
his brain was on fire,
songs he thought would take
a hundred years to write
suddenly aflame behind
his bulging eyes.

Dizzy in the barber's
chair, dizzy before
the chorus, dizzy
on the tennis court.

They did not believe him
even when he was adrift
in the first movement
of his Concerto in F.
He felt darkness beyond
the footlights seep
into his soul, nothing
but a sea of dream

everywhere, and heard
the echo of unplucked
strings, a quiver
of timpani dying out
quickly as one long
note from an oboe
wafted heavenward.
Then he found himself
back in Los Angeles,
familiar body still
upright on the piano stool,
Smallens with his baton
frozen at the shoulder,
only to blunder again
in the andante and they
told him nothing was wrong.

Dizzy in the Brown
Derby, dizzy before
the surf, dizzy
in the swimming pool.

They believed he was
not happy in Hollywood.
*There is nothing wrong
with Gershwin that a song
hit wouldn't cure.*
It was in his head, he was
lovelorn or he was riddled
with guilt, he was balding
and drooling, muddle-headed
by noon, listless underneath
the stars. They believed
him sapped by motion picture

making and longing for New
York City. Those hands
once a blur on the keyboard
could only move slow as flowers
toward the sun yet nothing
was wrong. In the spring
those sandaled feet
that could only shuffle
in the summer garden
had been quick as flame
to his own new music
yet nothing was wrong.

A blade of light
where the drawn shades
meet. Roses without odor,
icewater leaping from its cut
glass goblet, eyes leached
of luster in the shadowy
mirror of his brother's eyes.
He spread chocolates melted
in the oven of his palm
up his arms like an ointment,
and soon he was gone.

STARRY NIGHT

"Perhaps I might really recover if I were in the
country for a time."
—Vincent Van Gogh

Tonight the moon throbs with light
it seizes from stars as they rise
and the cypresses grow holy
before my eyes. Wind fills the sky.
I see clouds shudder, houses
and shops cower, but somehow
high grass finds its own source
of stillness. I think it is violet
in nature. Never has there
been such a night for seeing
how the dark world thrives
when day's brilliance dies
and sight fully becomes surprise.

Who would want all these deep blues
to soften as though toward dawn?
No dawn will bring along
a day as pure again. Who would
want to be well enough to lose
such hues? I know a man can
be so far from madness the true
world cannot find him. I know
he will be saved only when
the moon collects enough radiance
to render heaven tangible
as the breath of sunflowers.

Look: there is a glow inside
the emptiest spaces when we
study their darknesses. There is
also a hush no stroke of
a painter's brush can muffle.
Think of the instant swallows
rising above a field you enter
suddenly loop back in unison—
a thick landscape of faith
that is beyond words, yet explains
why I am standing here at all.

THE VIOLENCE OF THE DAWN

"There are ten dawns I would see again
—if I was able."
                    —Jack B. Yeats

Sky boiling sapphire from the sea
is flecked apple and carmine,
surging where it is shot through

with bolts of sun. The dark
shore and its claw of land
stand no chance against a dawn

drawn from earth's royal core.
This is a blue so deep it mauls
light and bursts white to the eye.

Now in the last moment Sligo Bay
can hold daybreak back, the cliff
crumbles its colors in a creamy

plunge the scored sea never seems
to notice. Close to shore, breakers
thicken and gleam. There is nothing

smooth or still about the way sunrise
lures mist and sheen from drenched
rocks or tames the tidal bulge.

This should be the first dawn
a man sees when he believes himself
free of memory. It will wash

over him like harsh ocean wind
but he will not turn away,
even when a young woman whose face

glows in the growing light
waves a bonnet the same raven
black the night leaves behind.

MENDELSSOHN AT 38

"On 1 November 1847, Mendelssohn's condition
rapidly deteriorated. He experienced the first of a
series of strokes."

—John O'Shea, from "The Mendelssohn Family"

I look back on the promise of my youth
(*Felix* the fortunate) and am so tired.
A boy in auburn ringlets playing fugues
for old Goethe, a boy with liquid fire
in his hands! I glimpsed myself in glacier
wind and flood waters under the slender
Devil's Bridge. I loved the wild allegro,
the clack of trains, wind in a seaside cave.
Swiss sunlight, Monti Albani's sweet air,
Loch Lomond. I found music everywhere.
Now some mornings I am too weak to fold
back my bedsheets. There is nothing I crave
as much as silence. Not even pine trees,
the rich smell of old stones with moss upon
them, or the sight of snowy peaks would please
me. Quiet, like the moment before song
stretched out forever. Stillness, that instant
before strings quiver. This is what I want.